D0083514

Princeton Studies in Muslim Politics

Dale F. Eickelman and Augustus Richard Norton, Editors

Diane Singerman, *Avenues of Participation: Family, Politics, and Networks in Urban Quarters of Cairo*

Tone Bringa, *Being Muslim the Bosnian Way: Identity and Community in a Central Bosnian Village*

Dale F. Eickelman and James Piscatori, *Muslim Politics*

Bruce B. Lawrence, *Shattering the Myth: Islam beyond Violence*

Ziba Mir-Hosseini, *Islam and Gender: The Religious Debate in Contemporary Iran*

Robert W. Hefner, *Civil Islam: Muslims and Democratization in Indonesia*

Muhammad Qasim Zaman, *The Ulama in Contemporary Islam: Custodians of Change*

Michael G. Peletz, *Islamic Modern: Religious Courts and Cultural Politics in Malaysia*

Oskar Verkaaik, *Migrants and Militants: Fun, Islam, and Urban Violence in Pakistan*

Laetitia Bucaille, *Growing up Palestinian: Israeli Occupation and the Intifada Generation*

Robert W. Hefner, editor, *Remaking Muslim Politics: Pluralism, Contestation, Democratization*

Lara Deeb, *An Enchanted Modern: Gender and Public Piety in Shiʿi Lebanon*

Roxanne L. Euben, *Journeys to the Other Shore: Muslim and Western Travelers in Search of Knowledge*

Loren D. Lybarger, *Identity and Religion in Palestine: The Struggle between Islamism and Secularism in the Occupied Territories*

Robert W. Hefner and Muhammad Qasim Zaman, eds., *Schooling Islam: The Culture and Politics of Modern Muslim Education*

Augustus Richard Norton, *Hezbollah: A Short History*

HEZBOLLAH

A Short History

Augustus Richard Norton

PRINCETON UNIVERSITY PRESS

PRINCETON AND OXFORD

Library of Congress Cataloging-in-Publication Data

Norton, Augustus R.
Hezbollah : a short history / Augustus Richard Norton.
p.   cm. — (Princeton studies in Muslim politics)
Includes bibliographical references and index.
ISBN-13: 978-0-691-13124-5 (hardcover : alk. paper)
ISBN-10: 0-691-13124-4 (hardcover : alk. paper)
1. Hizballah (Lebanon) 2. Lebanon—Politics and government—
1975–1990. 3. Lebanon—Politics and government—1990–
4. Shiites—Lebanon—Politics and government.
5. Islam and politics—Lebanon. 6. Geopolitics—Middle East. I. Title.
JQ1828.A98H6263 2007
324.25692′082—dc22
2006100594

British Library Cataloging-in-Publication Data is available

This book has been composed in Goudy and Avant Garde

Printed on acid-free paper. ∞

press.princeton.edu

Printed in the United States of America

3   5   7   9   10   8   6   4   2

Contents

Contents

Prologue

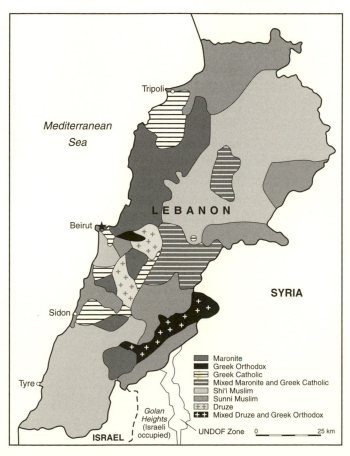

Map 1. Lebanon's major confessional groups (sects) and the areas where they predominate.

It was an easy summer evening in August 2004. The Shiᶜi Muslim village lies about five miles southeast of Tyre, Lebanon's southernmost city, and the border with Israel is eight miles due south. Al-Bazuriya boasts a few simple shops and a couple of hundred homes of stone or cinder block, and we are gathered on the large balcony of one of these homes. Grapes, begging for picking, hang overhead on a thick fabric of vines, shading a long table brimming with Lebanon's famous *mezze* (appetizers)—tabbouleh, hummus, pickles in pastel shades, finger-shaped wrapped grape leaves stuffed with rice and herbs, milk white cheese, breads, and other delicacies of vivid red, brown and orange hues. The *mezze* and the meats, fish, and chicken that would follow were to celebrate the visit of a son of the village of al-Bazuriya, a successful surgeon, and his bride, from Michigan. Many of the people around the table—parents, siblings, cousins, and friends—moved easily between Arabic and English, especially and most helpfully when this author lost his way in Arabic. English has been the preferred second language in almost every Lebanese Shiᶜi family for decades.

This is a successful middle-class Shiᶜi family, for which, like many others in Lebanon, education and emigration are the steps on a ladder to a good life. In other families and villages, the destinations would vary—Abidjan instead of Dearborn, Michigan; Ivory Coast instead of Brazil—but the pattern is the same. The Lebanese emigrants, whether their path of migration is circular, as with those who work in Africa as merchants and traders and return to Lebanon to marry and invest their earnings, or goes in one direction, as with those who end up in the Americas, typically sharing the largess they accumulate abroad with their extended families still in Lebanon. These remittances are vital to their families. By one credible estimate, the annual remittances of all Lebanese abroad totaled nearly $2.5 billion in 2001 (Hourani 2006, 27).

Over dessert and, later, small glasses of sweet hot tea, the conversation drifted from the cozy trivialities of family intimacy to serious talk about the politics of Lebanon now that the South was "liberated." A little more than four years before this gathering, in May 2000, Israel had withdrawn its occupation army from southern Lebanon under pressure from Lebanese fighters, especially the self-styled "Islamic Resistance" led by the Shiʿi Muslim Hezbollah (the "Party of God"). Mention of the two-decade-long Israeli occupation of their country and the retreat of the occupiers still inspired pride and a joyful *ilhamdililah* or *nushkur allah* ("praise to God" or "thank God") within this circle of family and friends. Like many Lebanese, this family, in the course of the 1990s, had come to believe that the Israelis might never leave.

These sons and daughters of Bazuriya wanted me to know that theirs was the village where Hasan Nasrallah, now the leader of Hezbollah, grew up and went to school. One of his teachers, who was present at the family gathering, recalled young Hasan's serious cast of mind and his piety even as an adolescent. Like many religiously minded young Lebanese Shiʿi men before him, Nasrallah went to study in the famous Shiʿi seminaries of Iraq's al-Najaf, one of the great shrine cities of Shiʿism. Nasrallah became secretary-general of Hezbollah in 1992, and ever since has been detested by Israel and America but widely admired in much of the Muslim world.

It was in al-Najaf as well as Karbala that key episodes in Shiʿism occurred, and multitudes of Shiʿa visit annually to pray there alongside the tombs of two of Shiʿism's epic figures. For Shiʿi Muslims, such as the young Nasrallah, the language, food, and hospitality of al-Najaf and Karbala were familiar. In contrast, the seminaries of Iran were further removed culturally, linguistically, and physically. Still, these days it is just as likely that scores of young Lebanese men will journey to Iran for their religious instruction than to Iraq. This is not so much because of a sudden new affinity for Iran but because Iraq, under Saddam Hussein, became a menacing place for Shiʿi students. Also, the country has been dangerous and chaotic since the Anglo-American invasion in March 2003. In any case, the Iranians offer an attractive stipend to entice young Shiʿa to their seminaries. One of the cousins, in fact, who was present on that summer evening in Bazuriya in 2004, was a pleasant young seminary student home for the summer from Qum in Iran. He was intent on welcoming a non-Arab visitor from America and eager to engage me in conversation, especially on the topic of his computer classes in Qum and the relative merits of Microsoft computer software.

In Bazuriya and villages across southern Lebanon, as in Shiʿi locales in and around Beirut and in the Beqaa valley, political affinities and loyalties are multilayered and constantly shifting. Although the parties on the secular left have lost their appeal for most of the Shiʿa, the secularist Communist party of Lebanon, with its emphasis on social and economic equity, retains pockets of fervent support. Some villages are renowned for the continuing grip of leftist ideologies (further to the east, the village of Kafr Rumann, for instance, is jokingly called "Kafr Moscow" by its neighbors). Traditional land-owning elites, who have held sway over their clients for nearly a century, retain pockets of support, especially when they are understood to have changed with the times and have cultivated reputations for fair dealing and honesty. But the two major political players are

5

now Amal, the reformist movement described in detail in chapter 1, and Hezbollah, the militant party introduced in chapter 2. Accurate membership figures are hard to find, but Amal, now more of an extensive patronage network than an institutionalized political party, clearly retains widespread support, especially in southern Lebanon. In fact, just down the street from the balcony dinner a large billboard commemorates ten Amal martyrs from Bazuriya who died fighting Israel. In contrast to Amal, Hezbollah enjoys broad-based support in all three areas where the Shiʿi Muslims predominate in Lebanon, namely, in the South, in Beirut and the vicinity of the city, and in the northern Beqaa valley and Hirmil region. Both these parties draw heavily on the rich history of Shiʿi Islam, especially the sect's famous martyrs and, in particular, Imam Hussein, the grandson of the Prophet Muhammad. This history is recounted in chapter 3.

Following the attack on the U.S. marine barracks in Beirut in 1983, Hezbollah has been associated with violence and terrorism in the minds of informed Americans. Chapter 4 addresses the broad question of violence with regard to Hezbollah and the implication that Hezbollah is a terrorist organization.

Over the last fifteen years Hezbollah has evolved from an Iranian-influenced conspiratorial terrorist group rejecting participation in Lebanese politics, to a party with considerable autonomy and a talent for playing politics and winning elections. The Shiʿi party is now part of the Lebanese government but simultaneously adopts an opposition demeanor, with a Janus-faced profile that infuriates detractors while seeming perfectly reasonable to its defenders and supporters. Chapter 5 describes and analyzes the organization's evolution and its complex profile on the Lebanese political landscape.

The pleasant summer evening described above marked an all-too-short period of calm in Lebanon's history. Just a few weeks later, Syria, Hezbollah's ally and the power broker in Lebanon, would force the extension in office of an unpopular president and trigger momentous developments in Lebanon and internationally. In the coming months a famous former prime minister would be blown to pieces by a bomb that also killed twenty-two of his colleagues. March 2005 saw nearly a million and a half people rise up in two massive demonstrations in Beirut streets, one condemning Syria for its likely role in the assassination, and the other praising Syria for its involvement in Lebanon.

In July 2006 Hezbollah launched an operation to capture two Israeli soldiers in Israel, thus provoking an Israeli invasion that would leave much of Hezbollah's constituency homeless and more than a thousand, predominantly Shi'i Muslim Lebanese dead in a war the Lebanese call Harb al-Tummuz ("the July war"). Hezbollah evidently had miscalculated, never anticipating Israel's furious onslaught. Although neither Israel nor Hezbollah were unequivocal victors, the war solidified Hezbollah's role as both a political player in Lebanon and a regional exemplar for other opposition-minded Muslims. How and why the war broke out when it did—after six years of relative calm on the Israeli-Lebanese border after the withdrawal of Israeli forces from southern Lebanon in 2000—is the subject of chapter 6.

Internal pressure on Hezbollah, once awash in praise and adulation for its leading role in forcing Israel's 2000 exit from Lebanon, now mounted to disarm its militia. France and the United States, working in rare unison under UN Security Council Resolution 1701, would support the fledgling Lebanese government and pressure Hezbollah to disarm. How the unexpected war of 2006, and its aftermath, will affect the course of Middle East history is still unclear, but the war certainly brought Hezbollah to the fore as a key influence on the region's political landscape. Hezbollah is not easily understood either by simplistic stereotypes that typically inform depictions of the organization in the newspapers and on the airwaves of the Western world nor by black and white worldviews. The purpose of this book is to offer a more balanced and nuanced account of this complex organization.

Chapter 1
Origins and Prehistory
of Hezbollah

Billboard in southern Lebanon depicting Musa al-Sadr, the seminal Shiʿi leader who disappeared in 1978; and Hasan Nasrallah, the Secretary-General of Hezbollah since 1992. Copyright A. R. Norton, 2006.

The modern state of Lebanon won its independence from France in 1943. The defining compromise of Lebanese politics was the *mithaq al-watani* or national pact, an unwritten understanding between the dominant political communities of the day—the Sunni Muslims and the Maronite Christians—that would provide the terms of reference for Lebanon's independence. In the 1920s the French, exploiting their League of Nations mandates in Lebanon and Syria, carved out generous chunks of Syria to create a viable "Greater Lebanon," thereby thwarting the Arab nationalist dream of an independent state in Damascus. For the Sunnis, the acceptance of an independent state ended the hope of reuniting Lebanon with Syria. Although the Sunnis, many of them merchants, dominated the new republic's coastal cities, their history was in the Syrian capital of Damascus. The Maronites, long the favored ally of French power and influence in the region, now had to concede that Lebanon was not an appendage of Europe but instead an Arab state. Neither Sunnis nor Christians spoke with a single voice, however, and dissent flourished.

The political system that emerged from the national pact was formalized into a system of sectarian communities, or confessions. Each of the country's seventeen recognized sects was accorded political privilege, including senior appointments in the bureaucracy, membership in parliament, and positions in high political office, roughly proportionate to the community's size.[1] This process was always rather

---

[1] At the end of the civil war the Copts became another recognized confession, bringing the total number to eighteen. The original seventeen included four Muslim sects: Sunni, Shi°a, °Alawi, and Druze; twelve Christian sects: Assyrians, Syriac Catholics, Syriac Orthodox, Chaldeans, Maronites, "Rome" Catholics, Greek Catholics, Greek Orthodox, Armenian Orthodox, Armenian Catholics, evangelicals, and smaller Christian sects, which are considered one group; and Jews (few

inexact, except for the highest political positions which were awarded to the Maronites, Sunnis, and Shiʿa. Thus, the Maronites, considered the plurality, were accorded the presidency, which carried preeminent prerogatives and powers, and the second largest community, the Sunnis, won the premiership, decidedly second fiddle to the presidency. The Shiʿi community, third largest, was awarded the speakership of the parliament, a position with far weaker constitutional powers than either the presidency or the premiership. The provenance of this allocation of power was a 1932 census of dubious reliability and, in fact, the last official census ever conducted in Lebanon. The data were sound estimates at best. The imbalance of power between the "three presidents" was rectified significantly by political reforms in 1989 in the agreement that provided the framework for ending the civil war of 1975–1990, which claimed about 150,000 lives.

The Shiʿi community, in any case, could yield little influence over the political system at the time, as it was impoverished and underdeveloped (Norton 1987, 16–23). A small community of Shiʿa lived in and around Beirut, but the overwhelming mass lived in southern Lebanon and in the northern Beqaa valley. Of course, the historical context for the impoverishment of all the Arab Shiʿi communities (found, notably, in Bahrain, Iraq, Kuwait, Lebanon, and Saudi Arabia) derives from the fact that the dominant Arab Sunnis often despised the Shiʿa for "deviating" from the path of Sunni Islam. Over the course of the Ottoman Empire, which ruled Lebanon and Syria more or less effectively for more than four hundred years, the Shiʿa were suspected

remain in Lebanon today, but children born of Lebanese Jewish parents may register as citizens at Lebanese embassies).

of being a stalking horse for Persia, notwithstanding the venerable origins of Arab Shiᶜism, which, in fact, long pre-dates the introduction of Shiᶜism in Persia in the sixteenth century. Indeed, the central contention between Shiᶜi and Sunni Muslims to this day goes back to the validity of the claim made by the partisans of ᶜAli, the husband of the Prophet Muhammad's daughter, Fatimah, that he should succeed Muhammad upon the prophet's death.

A conjuncture of social facts, regional conflicts, and do-mestic policies shaped the politicization of the Lebanese Shiᶜa in the 1950s, 1960s, and 1970s. The rate of this com-munity's natural increase outpaced all others in Lebanon, as the average Shiᶜi family generally had nine members in the early 1970s, whereas the average Christian household had only six. Although fertility among Sunni women was also higher than among the Christians, Shiᶜi women bore an av-erage of one more child than their fellow Muslims (Chamie 1981, 44). Families of a dozen or more children are not un-common among the Shiᶜa, and as mobility improved in the first decades of Lebanese independence, tens of thousands migrated from the hinterlands to Beirut and abroad.

The hardscrabble Shiᶜi farmers cultivated the hills and valleys of the South and the Beqaa plateau but most could not subsist on what they earned selling tobacco to the state monopoly or growing vegetables and fruits. Even those who owned land rather than working as a sharecropper often struggled to eke out a living from farming. The state was of little help, providing piddling sums for rural development, a pattern that still persists. In the northern Beqaa and the Hirmil region, where the influence of the state was espe-cially weak, poppies and hashish became valuable cash crops. In many Shiᶜi villages several generations of young men left Lebanon to find their fortunes in Ivory Coast, Nigeria, Senegal, and throughout Africa, as well as in Latin America and the Arab oil-producing states of the Gulf. Later, these migrant workers would return to Lebanon, sometimes with impressive sums of money, and usually with little affection for the traditionally powerful families that dominated Shiʿi society from Ottoman times.

In the South, the Shiʿi heartland, the influx of one hundred thousand Palestinians beginning with the 1948–49 Palestine war introduced a pool of cheap labor, willing to work for less than were Shiʿi farm laborers, adding further impetus to migration. Later, of course, following the civil war in Jordan in 1970–71, thousands of armed Palestinian guerrillas would move to Lebanon, where the Palestine Liberation Organization (PLO) would challenge the authority of the Beirut government and establish a virtual state-within-a-state encompassing west Beirut and much of southern Lebanon.

Against this background, the Lebanese Shiʿi Muslims mobilized their political efforts. For nearly half a century the transformation of this community from quiescence to activism has brought into question the durability of Lebanon's founding compromise, and substantially contributed to the violent turmoil that has enveloped the country in the 1970s and 1980s.

The Rise of Shiʿi Politics from the Mid-twentieth Century to the Lebanese Civil War

Political bosses (zuʿama) from a handful of powerful families dominated Shiʿi politics into the 1960s and maintained their control through extensive patronage networks. The authority of the zuʿama depended on their clients' support, but by the 1960s many young Shiʿi men and women became alienated from old-style politics and were attracted by new political forces. The promise of radical change could only have been irresistible to a community whose ethos emphasized its exploitation and dispossession by the ruling elites. In Lebanon, as in Iraq, Bahrain, Saudi Arabia, and Kuwait, Shiʿa in large numbers were attracted in the 1950s, 1960s, and 1970s to secular opposition parties. In Lebanon the opposition took the form of the Syrian Social Nationalist Party (SSNP), the Lebanese Communist Party (LCP), the Organization for Communist Labor Action, and pro-Syrian and pro-Iraqi factions of the Arab Socialist Baʿth (or "Resurrection") Party. Particularly in the case of the Communist organizations and the SSNP, there was an inherent ideological attraction to parties that condemned the tribal, religious, or ethnic bases of discrimination. Indeed, it is notable that the leadership of these secular parties was predominantly Christian. Although support for secular parties has dwindled, significant numbers of politicized Shiʿa continue to express a preference for them, usually in particular families, villages, or regions. For instance, the Communists remain strong in the large village of Braʿsheet in the South, in an area now otherwise dominated by Hezbollah, literally, the Party of God, and the Amal movement, an acroynym for Lebanese Resistance Detachments, often rendered as "Hope." Amal, and especially Hezbollah, were relative latecomers on the political scene and appealed to the Shiʿa in clearly sectarian terms, despite their avowals of welcoming all comers.

Four major (and sometimes intertwined) political trends distinguished the political mobilization of the Shiʿa after the 1960s: secularism, liberation—especially the view that the fate of the deprived Shiʿa was linked to the dispossessed Palestinians, Islamism, and reformism, often couched in demands for more access to political privilege and for stamping out corruption. Although Arab nationalism certainly enjoyed Shiʿi adherents, given that Sunni Muslims numerically dominate the Arab world, many of the Shiʿa would not see a unified Arab nation as a very ideal solution. In 1997 a fifth, incipient trend appeared from within Hezbollah, when Shaykh Subhi Tufayli, the organization's former secretary-general, launched a populist dissident movement in the Beqaa valley among alienated farmers and tribesmen. Although the fortunes of secular movements and parties have declined, the loyalties and sympathies of the Shiʿa remain widely distributed, and no single organization—including Hezbollah—may claim an overwhelming majority following from among the Shiʿa. By the 1990s, however, Hezbollah was certainly the best-organized political phenomenon and enjoyed the largest base of popular support.

Of the three distinctive trends preceding the emergence of Hezbollah in 1982, several secular parties, as well as the reformist Amal movement, retain a significant following. As the Lebanese civil war approached in the early 1970s and the armed Palestinian presence grew stronger, many young Shiʿa found their place in one or another of the *fidaʾi*, or guerrilla fighter organizations.[2] Support for the Palestinian cause has now withered but not disappeared. Political loyalties within families are often shared between two or more organizations or are not "lent" to any political group at all. Hussein Nasrallah, a brother of Hasan Nasrallah, a founding member of Hezbollah and its famous secretary-general, is a life member of Amal. When the two groups were at each other's throats in the late 1980s, Hussein was on the front

---

[2] *Fidaʾi* (pl., *fidaʾiyun*, rendered often as fedayeen) is a common Arabic term for one who sacrifices himself, that is, a guerrilla fighter.

lines confronting his brother. Notwithstanding the long-term commitments of the Nasrallah brothers, one commonly meets individuals whose biography includes membership in three or four different political organizations, usually in sequence. In Lebanon political support is conditional and political loyalty sometimes has a short shelf life. Even so, ideological currents have shifted dramatically in the last two decades in favor of Hezbollah, which offers an ideological vision that many Shiʿa now find persuasive.

The Palestine resistance movement did more than directly challenge the power of Lebanon's entrenched elites; the resistance fighters were also paid comparatively well. It is widely known that many young men, and a few women, took up arms not only out of an ideological commitment but also simply to feed their families in a society offering few other economic opportunities. Once full-fledged civil war erupted in 1975, the Shiʿa became the cannon fodder for the fedayeen. Indeed, more Shiʿa died in the fighting than members of any other sect.

Even before the Israeli invasion of 1982, the fortunes of the armed Palestinian presence had soured, especially in southern Lebanon where the Amal movement gained many adherents at the expense of the parties of the Left. Amal had been founded, in the early 1970s, by al-Sayyid Musa al-Sadr, the Iran-born cleric of Lebanese ancestry, as a militia adjunct to the Harakat al-Mahrumin, the Movement of the Deprived, the predominantly Shiʿi populist reform movement. Amal was initially trained by Fatah, the largest organization in the PLO, and played a minor role in the fighting of 1975 and 1976. Although Amal was aligned with the Lebanese National Movement (LNM)—an array of radical and reformist groups opposed to the political dominance

17

of the Maronite Christians—by 1976 the alignment was strained by Amal's support for Syria and its armed intervention to prevent a victory by the PLO and the LNM over the Maronite militias.

The Role of Musa al-Sadr

Musa Sadr, widely known as Imam Musa, was instrumental in improving the lot of the ordinary Shi‘a in southern Lebanon while reducing the power of traditional Shi‘i elites. His unremitting opponent was Kamil al-As‘ad, the powerful Shi‘i political boss from the southern town of al-Tayyiba who had long grown accustomed to power. Kamil-bey ("bey" is a Turkish honorific) accurately viewed al-Sadr as a serious threat to his political power base, which was built on a foundation of subordination and patronage. Physically imposing and a man of intelligence, courage, personal charm, enormous energy, and great complexity, al-Sadr attracted a wide array of supporters. He set out to establish himself as the paramount leader of the Shi‘i community. When he arrived in Lebanon in the late 1950s, the community was most known for its poverty and general underdevelopment.

Al-Sadr exhorted his followers not to accept their deprivation fatalistically; he believed that as long as his fellow Shi‘i could speak out through their religion they could overcome their condition. As he once observed, "Whenever the poor involve themselves in a social revolution it is a confirmation that injustice is not predestined" (Norton 1987, 40). One of his first significant acts was to establish a vocational institute in the southern town of Burj al-Shimali. The institute, constructed at a cost of about $165,000, became an important symbol of Musa al-Sadr's leadership, and it survives to this day under the competent supervision of his sister, known commonly as Sitt (or Sister) Rabab, one of the most admired woman in the Lebanese Shiʿi community.

Musa al-Sadr recognized the insecurity of the Maronites and acknowledged their need to maintain their monopoly hold on the presidency. Yet he was critical of this Christian community for its arrogant stance toward the Muslims, and particularly the Shiʿa. He argued that the Maronite-dominated government had neglected the South, where half the Shiʿa lived. He was anticommunist, probably not only on principled grounds but because the various Communist organizations were among his prime competitors for Shiʿi recruits. While the two branches of the Baʿth Party (pro-Iraqi and pro-Syrian) were making significant inroads among the Shiʿa of the South and of the Beirut suburbs, he appropriated their pan-Arab slogans. Although the movement he founded, Harakat al-Mahrumin and its Amal militia, was aligned with the ideologically eclectic and radical Lebanese National Movement in the early stages of the Lebanese civil war (1975–1976), he found its Druze leader, Kamal al-Jumblatt, irresponsible and exploitative of the Shiʿa and willing "to combat the Christians to the last Shiʿi" (Pakradouni 1983, 106).

Al-Sadr's stance toward the Palestinian presence in the South was similarly complex. He consistently expressed sympathy for Palestinian aspirations, and yet he was unwilling to countenance actions that exposed Lebanese citizens, especially Shiʿi citizens of the South, to additional suffering. Imam Musa prophetically warned the PLO that it was not in its interest to establish a state within a state in Lebanon. The PLO's failure to heed this warning helped to spawn the alienation of their "natural allies," the Shiʿa, who actively resisted the Palestinian fighters in their midst only a few years later. In May 1976 al-Sadr threw his support to Syria when Syrian president Hafez al-Asad intervened in Lebanon on the side of the Maronite militias and against the LNM and its Palestinian allies. Although he mistrusted Syrian motives in Lebanon and felt that it was only Lebanon's indigestibility that prevented it from being swallowed by its more powerful neighbor, he nonetheless believed that the Syrians were an important ally in his challenge to Palestinian power in the southern Lebanon.

Musa al-Sadr first came to prominence in 1969, when a Lebanese Supreme Islamic Shiᶜi Council came into existence with Imam Musa as its chairman. The Council, formally authorized two years earlier by the Chamber of Deputies, or Lebanese parliament, provided for the first time a representative body for the Shiᶜa independent of the Sunni Muslims. It was a stunning confirmation of al-Sadr's status as the leading Shiᶜi cleric and one of the most important political figures in the country. The al-Sadr–led Council quickly made its presence know by issuing demands in the military, social, economic, and political realms, including improved measures for the defense of the South, provision of development funds, construction and improvement of schools and hospitals, and an increase in the number of Shiᶜa appointed to senior government positions. Unfortunately the response of the Lebanese government was ineffectual. Its Council of the South (Majlis al-Janub), created in the late 1960s in the wake of a general strike organized by al-Sadr and chartered to support the development of the region, became an infamous locus of corruption.

The growing influence of Musa al-Sadr prior to the civil war certainly gave direction to the political awakening of the Shiᶜa; it bears reiterating, however, that Imam Musa led only a fraction of his politically affiliated co-religionists. It was the multi-confessional parties and militias that attracted the majority of Shi'i recruits and many more Shi'a carried arms under the colors of these organizations than under Amal. Perhaps al-Sadr's single most important success was to reduce the authority and influence of the traditional Shi'i elites, but it was the civil war and the associated explosion of extralegal organizations that smashed the power of many political personalities long comfortable in privilege and power.

Whatever he may have been, and despite his occasionally vehement histrionics, Musa al-Sadr was hardly a man of war. His weapons were words, and in a country where the force of arms increasingly held sway, his political efforts were eventually short-circuited. He seemed destined to be eclipsed by the violence that engulfed Lebanon.

In August 1978 al-Sadr flew from Beirut to Tripoli with two aides to attend ceremonies commemorating the ascent of Libyan leader Muammar Gaddafi to power in 1969. When his failure to arrive at the ceremony was noticed, rumors circulated that he had left for Italy. The Libyan government quickly claimed to have evidence that al-Sadr had indeed left the country. However, supporters of the missing cleric pointed out that al-Sadr's baggage was found in a Tripoli hotel and there was no evidence of his arrival in Rome. Airline crews could not confirm that al-Sadr had ever flown from Libya to Italy. Although his fate is unknown to this day, Gaddafi is widely suspected of having ordered his assassination because, so the rumors have it, he viewed him as a political rival.

The Resurgence of Amal

Amal which was fading into obscurity after the eruption of the civil war in 1975, began an impressive resurgence in part because of the intense Shi'i outcry after al-Sadr's enigmatic disappearance. Also contributing to Amal's renewed popularity was, of course, Israel's invasion of Lebanon in 1978 and the historic Iranian revolution of 1978–79, which provided an exemplar for action, if not a precise model for emulation.

Amal drew substantial support from the growing Shiʿi middle class, for whom the movement represented an assertive voice against the power of the political zuʿama. Equally important, Amal challenged the stifling and often brutal domination of the Palestinian guerrillas whose public support plummeted in the late 1970s and early 1980s for bringing southern Lebanon into the crossfire with Israel.

Israel's invasion of 1978, the "Litani Operation," though minor compared to the wars yet to come in 1982 and 2006, displaced hundreds of thousands of Lebanese from the southern region. Relations between the Shiʿa in the South and the Palestinian resistance and its Lebanese affiliates were deteriorating. Not only were the Shiʿa weary of being caught in the Israeli-Palestinian cross fire, but they increasingly viewed the Palestinians as an occupying force prone to high-handedness and brutality. Amal militiamen and Palestinian guerrillas clashed with increasing frequency. For most Amal supporters, the overriding and immediate concern was security, and their efforts were often centered on forming local home-guards or militias that, naturally, the PLO viewed with great suspicion. Fierce confrontations also erupted between Amal partisans and pro-Iraq groups, such as the Arab Baʿth (Resurrection) Party, the Nationalist Party, and the Iraq-sponsored Arab Liberation Front, given the Iraqi regime's often brutal treatment of Shiʿi Muslims.

Although Amal resistance fighters actively opposed the continuing Israeli occupation of Lebanon, especially after

1983, Amal tacitly welcomed the Israeli invasion of June 1982 because it broke the power of the Palestinian fighters in the South. Amal leaders, especially Nabih Berri and Daoud Suleiman Daoud, the powerful leader in the South until his assassination under still murky circumstances in the late 1980s, sought a modus vivendi with Israel and the United States. Berri's participation in the National Salvation Committee—which had been created by Lebanese president Elias Sarkis to foster dialogue among Lebanon's most powerful militia leaders during the Israeli siege of Beirut—was castigated by young radicals within Amal who described the Committee as no more than an "American-Israeli bridge" allowing the United States to enter and control Lebanon (Norton 1987, 105). There is no doubt that Berri's willingness to contemplate a deal that would favor Syria's enemies also provoked Damascus to lend support to Hezbollah as a counterweight to Amal.

Later, from 1985 to 1988, the militia and sympathetic units of the Lebanese army—spurred on by Syria—conducted its "war of the camps" to prevent the Palestinians from regaining the position of dominance they had enjoyed prior to the Israeli invasion. The campaign prompted Amal's emerging political rival among the Lebanese Shiʿa, Hezbollah, to assist the Palestinians. (The "war of the camps" is discussed further in chapter 4.)

As the civil war in Lebanon drew to a close in the late 1980s, Amal was overstretched and weakened. What had been a dynamic and progressive movement in the early 1980s, with extensive popular support, now became a full-blown patronage system with all the corruption, inefficiency, and inequity that Amal had long ascribed to the traditional Zuʿama. As for Nabih Berri, with the end of the internal war in 1990 he became speaker of the parliament and remains a fixture in Lebanese politics. The irony of Berri's transformation from populist nemesis of the confessional system to powerful and wealthy denizen of confessional politics is not lost on the Lebanese.

After Imam Musa's disappearance, the Supreme Islamic Shiʿi Council was taken over by the cerebral Shiʿi ʿalim,[3] Shaykh Muhammad Mahdi Shams al-Din, an intellectually gifted cleric without a significant grass-roots following. Under his guidance, however, the Council became especially active in sponsoring and launching a series of ecumenical dialogues, intended to foster dialogue between Christians and Muslims. Shams al-Din emphasized the spiritual renewal of Muslims rather than the goal of seeking power, which, he argued, is often at cross purposes with the goal of Islamic renewal. Although it still enjoys respect as a religious and political focal point of the growing Shiʿi professional class, it has been eclipsed both by Amal and Hezbollah, especially since Shams al-Din's death from lung cancer in 2001. Today the group is led by the plain-spoken cleric and Amal's longtime ally ʿAbd al-Amr Qabalan, the Jaʿfari Mufti al-Mumtaz, that is, the officially recognized senior expert on Shiʿi religious law. This author was first introduced to him, in fact, in 1980 by the Amal leader in the South,

---

[3] The term ʿalim (pl., ʿulama), which literally means "scholar," connotes a person who has acquired specialized religious knowledge, whether in philosophy, jurisprudence, or rhetoric, or who has profound knowledge of the Quran. Although it is convenient to think of an ʿalim as a cleric or member of the clergy, this is only an approximation, as the ʿalim may not necessarily hold any formal religious position, and there is no close equivalent to the concept of ordination in Islam. In Christianity, a "man of religion" is often understood to be a member of the clergy, whereas in Islam a "rajul al-tadayyun" means, literally, a religious man, not an ʿalim.

Daoud Suleiman Daoud, at an informal Amal gathering in a Shi'i village. Qabalan, tellingly, remains the vice president of the Council; the post of president is vacant. Although the Council no longer has the extensive popular support it had during its years under al-Sadr's leadership, it does enjoy guaranteed access to the state and remains a potential institutional rival to Amal, as well as to Hezbollah.

Chapter 2
The Founding of Hezbollah

A view of southern Lebanon, where Hezbollah and the Amal movement compete for support. Copyright A. R. Norton, 2006.

The late 1970s and early 1980s were a time of great foment, enthusiasm, and transition among the Shiʿa of
Lebanon. Amal, as noted in chapter 1, enjoyed a resurgence
among the Shiʿa of southern Lebanon, particularly following the disappearance of Sayyid Musa al-Sadr in Libya in
August 1978 and the example set by the Shiʿa-led Islamic
Revolution in Iran in 1978–79. Originally an adjunct militia
to the Movement of the Deprived, Amal expanded into a
political reform movement as well, and its new leaders were
not clerics but members of the lay middle class, typified by
the lawyer Nabih Berri, who became leader in 1979. Berri's
father, Mustafa, had been a trader in Sierre Leone, one of
thousands of Shiʿa who had left Lebanon to seek opportunities in Africa. (Nabih was born in Freetown, Sierre Leone's
capital.)

In the early 1980s Amal embraced many ideological currents and disagreements and had no firm hierarchy. What
most adherents of the movement shared was a disdain for
the *zuʿama* (political bosses), who traditionally dominated
Shiʿi society, and anger toward Palestinian guerrillas and
their allies. Although one heard expressions of hatred toward Israel, particularly in the South, these were far less
common and less intense than they became a quarter-cen-
tury later.

Amal officials at the time would speak with admiration of
Iranian intellectuals such as ʿAli Shariati, the Paris-trained
Iranian modernist and intellectual who urged Muslims to
avoid becoming "humanoids" uncritically emulating the
West. Shariati, who died in 1977 and was buried in Damascus, with a eulogy delivered by his friend Musa al-Sadr, exhorted his multitude of readers and listeners to find their
identity in Islam, especially in the exemplary courage of the
prophet Muhammad's grandson, Hussein, whose martyrdom

in 680 c.e. or 10 a.h. (discussed in chapter 3) became the model for the Iranian Revolution. Mehdi Barzargan, head of Iran's Freedom Movement and revolutionary Iran's first prime minister, was also accorded great respect, as was Mustafa Chamran, a close associate of Imam Musa who earned his engineering Ph.D. from the University of California, Berkeley. Each of the three was a noted reformer, but Barzargan was pushed aside in Iran as the revolution grew more radical, and Chamran, who became chair of the Supreme Defense Council in Iran, died under mysterious circumstances in a plane crash on the Iraqi front in the first year of the eight-year Iran-Iraq War (1980–88).

The Iraq Connection

Amal officials also spoke with deep respect for Imam Musa's Iraqi cousin Ayatollah Muhammad Baqr al-Sadr of al-Najaf, the Iraqi cleric who suffered summary execution in Iraq, in April 1980, after he was forced to watch the rape and murder of his sister. In May 1980, when the author arrived in southern Lebanon, the horrid killing of Baqr al-Sadr was often discussed, usually coupled with a denunciation of Iraq—and its Lebanese allies. Baqr al-Sadr was a major thinker whose books in Arabic, particularly *Iqtisaduna* (Our Economy) are revered as seminal. (His nephew, of course, is Muqtada al-Sadr, the young firebrand who formed the Jaysh al-Mahdi [the "Army of the Guided One"] in Iraq after Saddam Hussein's Ba'thist regime was toppled in 2003.) In my visits with middle-class Amal supporters and officials, in 1980 and 1981 and many times later, I often spotted Baqr al-Sadr's books on a bookshelf, but perhaps more as an emblem of respect than as a volume that actually had been read. In Lebanese Shi'i villages, in those early chaotic days, posters honoring Baqr al-Sadr were almost as widespread as those featuring Musa al-Sadr, which far outnumbered images of Ayatollah Khomeini.

When young Lebanese Shiʿi men were selected for a religious education, their traditional destinations had been the revered Shiʿi seminaries of al-Najaf or Karbala in Iraq. By the end of the 1970s, however, as the revolution in Iran gathered force, Iraq had become inhospitable for foreign Shiʿa. In 1978 Ayatollah Khomeini was himself expelled from Iraq at the insistence of the Shah, thereby gaining international notoriety in a suburb of Paris with much of the international media just a few steps away as the Iranian revolution gathered force. Young Lebanese Shiʿi clerics such as Subhi Tufayli and ʿAbbas Musawi, who later played important leadership roles in Hezbollah's early days, trickled back into Lebanon from Iraq. Musawi established a *hawza*,[1] or religious seminary, in Baalbak, where the future Hezbollah leader Seyyid Hasan Nasrallah became his student and protégé. The returnees from Iraq brought with them revolutionary fervor and the commitment to change their societies. They shared antipathy toward Israel and loyalty to Iran. Most of the returnees were members of the Hizb al-Daʿwa party ("Party of the [Islamic] Call"), founded in Iraq in 1958 as an Islamic alternative to the Communist Party. The Lebanese Daʿwa was disbanded, and its erstwhile members were instructed by party strategists to infiltrate the secular Amal and reform it from within. Sayyid Muhammad Hussein Fad-

---

[1] In the Iraqi or Iranian context, *hawza* refers to a complex of seminaries roughly resembling a university with affiliated colleges, as in the al-Najaf *hawza* led in 2006 by Ayatollah ʿAli Sistani. In Lebanon, in contrast, *hawza* refers to a single seminary. Ruha Jurdi Abisaab, a leading authority on the topic, reports that, in the 1990s, there were sixteen hawzas in Lebanon with about six hundred scholars enrolled (Abisaab 2006).

lallah urged them in the same direction—away from Amal's de facto secularism toward something approximating an Islamic system of rule (Sankari 2005 172). After Musa al-Sadr's disappearance in 1978, Fadlallah was the most influential ʿalim in Lebanon.

Iranian revolutionaries, meanwhile, had long been familiar with Lebanon. Many, including Mohsen Rafiqdost, who became the head of the Pasdaran or Revolutionary Guards, had trained in the Beqaa valley of Lebanon with the PLO. This is a prime reason for the extraordinarily enthusiastic reception that Yasser Arafat enjoyed in Teheran, in February 1979, just weeks after the triumphant return of Khomeini. Arafat was handed the keys to the Israeli Embassy, among other honors.

For its part, Syria, in the early 1980s, had a very different future in mind. It saw in Amal a mechanism for checking Palestinian power in Lebanon, especially if Arafat should seek his own route to peace, deserting Syria. By 1980 and 1981 young Amalists were going off to train in Syria and coming back wearing new, Syria-style uniforms and sporting military-style radios. As tensions between Amal and the Palestinians worsened in 1981 and 1982, many expected a war—but not with Israel. Some leading Amal figures even argued that they were in an objective alliance with Israel against Palestinian guerrillas.

The 1982 Israeli Invasion

Israel invaded Lebanon on June 5, 1982, following an eleven-month cease-fire with the PLO, which Israel claimed had been broken by the attempted assassination of the Israeli ambassador to the United Kingdom Shlomo Argov, who had been badly wounded but survived. It made little difference to the Israelis that the assassination had been carried out by a renegade Palestinian group led by the infamous Sabri al-Banna ("Abu Nidal"), a blood foe of the PLO. The invasion gave Ariel Sharon, then the Israeli defense minister, carte blanche to pursue his own dream of destroying the PLO as a political force in the region and putting in place a pliant government in Beirut that would become the second Arab state, after Egypt, to enter into a formal peace agreement with Israel (Schiff and Yaari 1984). Within the Israeli government at the time—as within the American foreign policy establishment—there was little understanding of the developments under way among the Shiʿi Muslims of Lebanon and no analysis was made of the impact of this invasion on them.

Even if Israel had not launched its invasion of southern Lebanon in 1982, the young would-be revolutionaries among the Shiʿa would have pursued their path of emulating Iran's Islamic revolution. Undoubtedly, however, the invasion pushed the Shiʿa further in this direction, creating conditions for the establishment and flourishing of Hezbollah. The former Israeli prime minister Ehud Barak put the matter succinctly in July 2006: "When we entered Lebanon . . . there was no Hezbollah. We were accepted with perfumed rice and flowers by the Shia in the south. It was our presence there that created Hezbollah" (*Newsweek*, July 18, 2006). As Barak's comment suggests, by occupying Lebanon rather than promptly withdrawing, Israel wore out is warm welcome and provided a context for Hezbollah to grow.

Another Israeli prime minister, Yitzhak Rabin, who was assassinated in 1995, made precisely the same point in 1987, speaking of how Israel had let the "genie out of the bottle."[2] When Rabin asked to see me in December 1984, I urged

---

[2] Yitzhak Rabin made this comment a number of times, including on the British Grenada Productions documentary film *The Sword of Islam* (1987). He also made the comment to me in a meeting in New York City, but I do not recall the year.

him to leave Lebanon because a continued Israeli presence would inevitably radicalize the Shi°i community. He replied, to the best of my recollection, "Professor, I am a politician, and what will I say to the people of Kiryat Shimona when the rockets fall?"[3] And so the die was cast.

Hezbollah Emerges

Although its leading members refer to 1982 as the year the group was founded, Hezbollah did not exist as a coherent organization until the mid-1980s. From 1982 through the mid-1980s it was less an organization than a cabal. The Lebanese who comprised its first cadre were young, committed revolutionaries, in some cases barely in their twenties. Sayyid Hasan Nasrallah, who was only twenty-two in 1982, had been a rising star in his teens as an Amal representative in al-Bazuriya, his village in southern Lebanon. His mentor, thirty-year-old Sayyid °Abbas al-Musawi, from Nabisheet in the Beqaa valley, had taken him under his wing in al-Najaf in 1982, at the direction of Baqr al-Sadr. Raghib Harb, also thirty years old at the time of the Israeli invasion, was born in Jibsheet in the South. Harb, a major early leader of the resistance in the South, would be assassinated, probably by Israel, in 1984. And Shaykh Subhi Tufayli, a firebrand from Brital outside Baalbak, who would become Hezbollah's first secretary-general in 1989, was only thirty-four in 1982.

Iran and Syria share credit for sponsoring these young revolutionaries, although Iran certainly played the leading role. For Iran, the creation of Hezbollah was a realization of the revolutionary state's zealous campaign to spread the message of the self-styled "Islamic revolution." From Syria's

---

[3] The author would like to thank Professor Yossi Kostiner of Tel Aviv University for reminding him of this meeting.

standpoint, the new militant Shi'i party was a fortuitous instrument for preserving Syrian interests: supporting Hezbollah allowed Syria to maintain its alliance with Iran, gain the means for striking indirectly at both Israel and the United States, and keep its Lebanese allies, including the Amal movement, in line.

But Syria's support of the young Shi'i militants was ambivalent. The 1980s were rocky times in Syria's relations with Iran, and the al-Asad regime in Damascus remained wary of Hezbollah and its ties to the Islamic republic for a full decade. While maintaining its rapport with Hezbollah throughout the 1980s, Damascus also reinforced its ties to Amal. The U.S. government unwittingly aided Syria in this tactic when Amal's political overtures to Washington, in 1982, yielded little benefit.

Syria has no overall interest in seeing Amal or Hezbollah (or any other political force) triumph in Lebanon, and its strategy in Lebanon has consistently followed the principles of Realpolitik. To paraphrase the dictum of Lord Palmertson, Syria has neither eternal allies nor perpetual enemies in Lebanon. The Hezbollah leadership understands this and maintains its strategic alliance with Damascus, ever mindful that alliances of convenience are expendable by definition.

The Hezbollah Worldview

Notwithstanding this Syrian connection, throughout the 1980s Hezbollah hewed closely to the Iranian line. In fact, its remarkable programmatic document of 1985, an open letter addressed to the "Downtrodden in Lebanon and in the World," bears a strong made-in-Tehran coloration (translation in Norton 1987, 167–87).[4] This remarkable

---

[4] The page references in the text below are to the translation in Norton 1987, 167–87.

document emphasized that the 1978–79 revolution in Iran served as an inspiration to action, a proof of what can be accomplished when the faithful gather under the banner of Islam. "We address all the Arab and Islamic peoples to declare to them that the Muslim's experience in Islamic Iran left no one any excuse since it proved beyond all doubt that bare chests motivated by faith are capable, with God's help, of breaking the iron and oppression of tyrannical regimes" (183–84). "It is time to realize that all the Western ideas concerning man's origin and nature cannot respond to man's aspirations or rescue him from the darkness of misguidedness and ignorance" (184). Islam is the answer. "Only Islam can bring about man's renaissance, progress, and creativity because 'He lights with the oil of an olive tree that is neither Eastern nor Western, a tree whose oil burns, even if not touched by fire, to light the path. God leads to His light whomever He wishes'" (184).

Hezbollah released this revealing 1985 document to mark the first anniversary of the assassination of Shaykh Raghib Harb, the bright young cleric of Jibsheet in southern Lebanon. It declares that the world is divided between the oppressed and the oppressors, the latter being "the countries of the arrogant world"—especially the United States and the Soviet Union (still Cold War adversaries in 1985)—who struggle for influence at the expense of the Third World. "Consequently, the oppressed countries have become the struggle's bone of contention and the oppressed peoples have become its fuel" (178). In Iran the ethos of the revolution was summed up by the slogan "neither East nor West," which is also Hezbollah's view. One commentator, writing in the Hezbollah newspaper al-ʿAhd, puts the two superpowers on the same plane: "The Soviets are not one iota different from the Americans in terms of political dan-

ger, indeed are more dangerous than them in terms of ideological considerations as well, and this requires that light be
shed on this fact and that the Soviets be assigned their
proper place in the forces striving to strike at the interests
of the Moslem people and arrogate their political present
and future" (al-ʿAhd, May 9, 1987, 12). Within Lebanon,
Hezbollah proved to be especially intolerant of the Communist Party. Dozens, if not hundreds, of party members were
killed in a brutal, bloody campaign of suppression and assassination in 1984 and 1985.

The starring role for Islam's main enemy, according to
the Hezbollah document, went to the United States, which
was charged with using its "spearhead," Israel, to directly
or indirectly inflict suffering upon the Muslims of Lebanon
(179). "Imam Khomeini, the leader, has repeatedly stressed
that America is the reason for all our catastrophes and the
source of all malice. By fighting it, we are only exercising
our legitimate right to defend our Islam and the dignity of
our nation" (170).

The French were also attacked, largely because of their
long-standing support of the Maronite community in Lebanon, and for their arms sales to Iraq. In August 1989, for
example, the Hezbollah radio station noted that the French
should be "taught a lesson because of their scorn for other
people and lack of respect for Lebanese Muslims" (International Herald Tribune, August 24, 1989).

In Hezbollah's worldview, compromise and mediation
were no answer. Where fractiousness existed among Muslims, it had to have been the product of imperialism. Dis-
unity was caused by imperialism and its agents, including
compromisers, evil ʿulama, and the leaders imposed by colo-
nialism (184). It followed, then, that the Lebanonese government was corrupt to its core. No renovation could make

it palatable, and those who pursued such solutions were trai-
tors to Islam. Self-help was the only answer. The superpowers were corrupt. They had no answers for Lebanon. When
the Muslims were under brutal attack in 1982, no one came
to their rescue. "We appealed to the world's conscience but
heard nothing from and found no trace of it" (170). The
United Nations, despite its pretensions, merely served the
interests of the arrogant superpowers or was, at least, prevented from acting by the tacit conspiracy of the superpowers through their use of the veto. The only answer was to
fight under the banner of Islam. "Thus, we have seen that
aggression can be repelled only with the sacrifice of blood,
and that freedom is not given but regained with the sacrifice
of both heart and soul" (171).

Hezbollah thus positioned itself as a force resisting the
actions of Israel and the superpowers, which have led to
subjugation and oppression throughout the Third World.
The objective was to free Lebanon from the manipulation
and chicanery of the malevolent outside powers in order to
achieve "the final departure of America, France, and their
allies from Lebanon and the termination of the influence of
any imperialist power in the country" (173).

One of the burdens of the open letter was to explain and
justify Hezbollah's use of violence, which, it is argued, the
West trivialized as "a handful of fanatics and terrorists who
are only concerned with blowing up drinking, gambling, and
entertainment spots" (170). "Each of us is a combat soldier
when the call of *jihad* demands it and each of us undertakes
his task in the battle in accordance with his lawful assign-
ment within the framework of action under the guardianship of the leader jurisprudent" (169).

Hezbollah regards negotiations with Israel as only a form
of compromise that validates Israel's occupation of Pales-

tine. "We condemn strongly all the plans for mediation between us and Israel and we consider the mediators a hostile party because their mediation will only serve to acknowledge the legitimacy of the Zionist occupation of Palestine" (179). The ultimate objective is to destroy Israel and to liberate Palestine. Thus "Israel's final departure from Lebanon is a prelude to its final obliteration from existence and the liberation of venerable Jerusalem from the talons of occupation" (173). This absolutism explains the operational links between Hezbollah and the rejectionist Palestinian groups that have opposed the efforts of mainstream PLO officials to make peace with Israel.

A key unanswered question in the letter is, precisely, Hezbollah's political design for Lebanon, a significant omission in view of that organization's expressed disdain for the existing political system. The letter only states that, once Lebanon is freed from external and internal domination, the Lebanese will be allowed to determine their fate; if they choose freely, they will only choose Islam. Whether the goal is clerical rule under the concept of the *wilayat al-faqih*, the creation of an Islamic republic on the Iranian model, is not made clear in the open letter. Some scholars claim that Hezbollah was not calling for "guardianship" on the Iran model but rather the "rule of the *shariʿa*," or Islamic law, but this would be a distinction without difference.

The application of *shariʿa* in the context of Khomeini's neo-Shiʿism requires clerical guardianship. In any event, given the doctrinal role of the *mujtahids*, clerics qualified to independently interpret religious law and responsibility, and the requirement of *taqlid* (imitation) in Shiʿi Islam, a state founded on the *shariʿa* could scarcely function without regular recourse to the *mujtahids*. In Shiʿi Islam, in the absence of the Awaited Imam (Imam al-Muntazar), the adherent must "imitate" (*taqlid*) the legal rulings of the *muj-tahids*. This is the doctrinal foundation for the influence of the clerics in Shiʿism, in contrast to the more fluid conception of religious authority held by Sunni Islam. For both Sunni and Shiʿi Muslims, Islam is a system of law, and individuals have been known to "convert" from one legal school to another or from one clerical authority to another, in order to exploit a more advantageous legal interpretation. Thus a former prime minister of Lebanon, Salim al-Huss, a Sunni Muslim, performed a technical one-day conversion to Shiʿism in order to improve inheritance rights for his daughters under the Shiʿi Jaʿfari legal interpretation. Shiʿi inheritance rules are more favorable to daughters than the Sunni schools of law.

The open letter also addresses the role of the ʿulama, implicitly the bulk of the Sunni ʿulamas as well as those Shiʿi clerics who do not actively support Hezbollah: "Therefore, one of your most important responsibilities, O Muslim ʿulama, is to educate the Muslims to abide by the dictates of Islam, to point out to them the political line they should follow, to lead them toward glory and honor, and to devote attention to the religious institutes so that they may graduate leaders faithful to God and eager to uphold religion and the nation" (186). "We do not hide our commitment to the rule of Islam and that we urge an Islamic system that alone guarantees justice and dignity for all and prevents any new imperialist attempt to infiltrate our country" (173). Hezbollah advocates "adoption of the Islamic system on the basis of free and direct selection by the people, not the basis of forceful imposition, as some people imagine" (175). Unfortunately the organization's history of violence against its political and ideological rivals casts doubt on Hezbollah's commitment to voluntarism. Anecdotal data from non-affiliated

Shi'a living in the Hezbollah-dominated regions only deepened these doubts.

The letter had been issued at a time of real exultation born from a string of military and political successes that humiliated both the United States and Israel. Hezbollah had played a major role in the departure of the American marines from Lebanon and the scuttling of the U.S.-brokered May 17, 1983, agreement between Lebanon and Israel, and the organization held the world at bay over the fate of Western hostages, the last hostage not released until 1991. Equally impressive was that it forced an Israeli withdrawal from most of Lebanese territory. In January 1985, only a month before the letter was issued, Israel announced its decision to "redeploy" its forces and then retreated to the border region where its self-declared "security zone" became a magnet for Hezbollah attacks that continued through the 1990s (Norton 1993).

Implementing the Design

True to the often intransigent and consistently militant tone of the open letter, Hezbollah moved aggressively, in the mid- to late 1980s, to strike at Westerners in Lebanon and at Western influence. Groups linked to Hezbollah, if not directly controlled by the party, kidnapped dozens of foreigners and held them hostage for as long as seven years (in the case of the American journalist Terry Anderson). Although the myriad groups that abducted foreigners often pursued their own local agendas, particularly the freeing of Lebanese held in Kuwaiti and Israeli prisons, the captors were also sensitive to the interests and influence of Iran. As a result, freeing captives required a complex series of negotiations involving the release of Iranian assets frozen by the United

States, the release of Lebanese prisoners held by Israel, and, more important, a government in Tehran determined to end the hostage crisis. Negotiations were conducted under the personal auspices of UN Secretary-General Perez de Cuellar, and, by the early 1990s, Iranian officials (not least, President Hashim Rafsanjani) clearly wished to resolve the issue. President George H. W. Bush's January 1989 inaugural promise that "goodwill begets goodwill" created a mood of expectancy in Tehran.

Even so, long, tedious negotiations were required between Perez de Cuellar's representative, Giandominico Picco, and the captors themselves. At that point in Lebanon's history, the civil war had drawn to a close, most Lebanese did not support the taking of hostages (few ever did), and the conclusion of the Cold War was pregnant with potential to redefine the dimensions of politics in the region. Picco's valuable book, *Man with a Gun*, presents an insider's account of negotiations that were often as much between the captors as with their Italian interlocutor. Picco does not hide his disappointment that the United States did not, in the end, return goodwill for goodwill in terms of reciprocating Iranian efforts to free the hostages (Picco 1999).

Perhaps the signal act of the period was the June 1985 skyjacking of TWA flight 847 to Beirut, masterminded by the infamous Imad Mughniyah, who continues to be linked to Hezbollah's External Security Organization. Hezbollah was deeply implicated in the hijacking, which was intended to highlight the fate of 766 Lebanese prisoners held in Israel (primarily in the Atlit prison), many of whom languished in extremely difficult conditions, with no recourse to the protections of international law. Some of the captives had participated in resistance operations, but others were merely suspects that Israel held hostage.

The hijacking exposed the deep tensions between Hezbollah and Amal, for when Amal leader Nabih Berri attempted to mediate the crisis, Hezbollah heatedly objected that Berri had no ability to speak on its behalf. The crisis ended only when Israel quietly agreed to release Lebanese prisoners from the Atlit prison, and Syria, and especially when Iranian Speaker Hashemi Rafsanjani, intervened to pressure the perpetrators to bring the crisis to an end.

By then there was much tension between Amal and Hezbollah, which finally exploded in 1988–89, with two militias fighting to win the Shiʿi heartland in the South, as well as the teeming southern suburbs of Beirut, where fully half the Shiʿi population resides. The fighting was sparked by the kidnapping of U.S. marine Lt. Colonel William R. Higgins, who was serving with UN forces in the south. The operation was carried out by a splinter group of Amal—the "Believers' Resistance," led by the former Lebanese army intelligence sergeant Mustafa Dirani—a group sympathetic to Hezbollah. Dirani himself was later kidnapped by Israeli forces from his Beqaa valley village in 1994 and released in 2004 in a prisoner exchange (more on this in chapter 4).

The Higgins incident threatened Amal's strategy of maintaining a cooperative working relationship with the UNIFIL (United Nations Interim Force in Lebanon), so Amal reacted by attempting to find Higgins and free him. The kidnappers evaded the Amal searchers, and Higgins was later brutally murdered, but not before the incident triggered serious clashes between Amal and Hezbollah, allowing Amal to momentarily consolidate its grip on southern Lebanon. Shortly thereafter, in the fall of 1988, fighting erupted in the southern suburbs of Beirut, and Amal was badly defeated, losing virtually its entire military foothold in the capital. Hezbollah's efforts to roll back Amal influence in the South, in 1989, succeeded in eroding Amal's position there, though Amal remains popular in the South.

Hezbollah certainly served as a stalking horse for Iranian interests, especially in the 1980s, but by the end of the decade Iran's policies were changing—often in ways unsettling to devotees of the Islamic revolution—and its support for Hezbollah wavered. In 1988 the first Gulf war, which Ayatollah Khomeini had vowed to pursue until Saddam Hussein was toppled, ended with Iran embracing a ceasefire. Iran's submission inspired sarcastic graffiti in Lebanon: "Why 598 and not 425?" a reference to UN Security Council Resolution 598 that ended the war and Resolution 425 that dealt with the restoration of security in southern Lebanon. With Khomeini's death in 1989, this charismatic symbol of the revolution was replaced by men of more modest views who now had to address the mundane but daunting challenges of restoring post-revolutionary Iran. The Iranian president Ali Akbar Hashemi Rafsanjani and the new Iranian leadership of the early 1990s moved to reorient their policy more toward the broader Shi'i community and Lebanon as a whole, distancing themselves from militias, at least for a few years (Norton 1990, 132). Internecine fighting between Amal and Hezbollah had provoked a significant change of attitude in Tehran, where the bloodletting in Lebanon was viewed with disgust. Because the vicious fighting between the two groups cost many civilian lives, Rafsanjani reacted sharply, pointedly condemning both sides for their actions. But Iran was not merely outraged at the bloodshed in Lebanon, for 1990 marked the closing days of the Cold War, the assembling of an international coalition against Iraq's invasion of Kuwait, and the long overdue end of the Lebanese civil war. Thus Iran was adjusting to the new balance of power in the world in which U.S. power was without rival.

Hezbollah, from its first moments, had always defined itself in contrast to Amal. The coterie of young clerics who made up Hezbollah's cadre in the 1980s and early 1990s resented Amal's non-clerical leadership and accommodation with Lebanese clientelism. Unlike the Amal politicos, who were intent on comprising the new Shiʿi bourgeoisie, the leaders of Hezbollah—brimming with revolutionary passion—refused to accommodate a corrupt political system, or so they said in the 1980s. Most of them had been trained in Najaf, Karbala, and Qum where they were ideologically inculcated by Muhammad Baqir al-Sadr, Muhsin al-Hakim, and Ruhollah al-Musavi Khomeini, but by the 1990s their fervor began to give way to a more realistic sense of the possible.

In contrast to the fierce ideological tenor in the 1985 open letter, Hezbollah now pragmatically confronted the shifting political landscape of regional politics, as well as the changing terrain of Lebanese politics. The result has been the evolution to a Janus-faced organization, retaining a fierce commitment to confront Israel's occupation in southern Lebanon while engaging in precisely the game of confessional Lebanese politics that they previously had denounced. Hezbollah was affected by the change in the Iranian regime, especially after the death of Ayatollah Khomeini in 1989, as well as by Syria's growing political and military dominance in Lebanon. Meantime, there is little doubt that Hezbollah has proved responsive to the attitudes and aspirations of its domestic constituency. This constituency includes a large portion of the expanding Shiʿi middle class that grew skeptical of the Amal movement and its corruption, and came to admire Hezbollah's relative integrity.

The party's broadened constituency brings with it new requisites for sustaining support, as the new Shiʿi middle class does not yearn to live in an Islamic Republic, least of all the Islamic Republic of Lebanon. Hezbollah's virtue aside, it frequently cites its goal to be an open political system with a place at the table of government, instead of standing as a supplicant at the back door of politics. There have been periodic hints from leading Hezbollah officials, including Nasrallah and Deputy Secretary-General Naʿim Qassem, that the 1985 open letter is obsolete and no longer an authoritative guide to the party's positions. This issue was the topic of a documentary on al-Jazeera TV, in September 1998, where a number of party officials, members, supporters, and journalists were interviewed for the program (Alagha 2006, 328). The conclusion reached was that the open letter belonged to a certain historical moment that had passed. Hezbollah officials, in various settings in Lebanon, have made the same point to this author. Still, the bald fact is that the 1985 program has not been explicitly replaced. The result is that skeptics and opponents of the party are left with a picture of ambivalence and, perhaps, dissimulation, which have only been sharpened by Hezbollah's behavior in the early twenty-first century.

Chapter 3

Being a Shi`i Muslim in the Twentieth Century

A museum in the village of Nabisheet, in the Beqaa valley, commemorates the Hezbollah martyrs who have died in southern Lebanon fighting Israel. The village is the birthplace of `Abbas al-Musawi, the Secretary-General of Hezbollah, who was assassinated, along with his wife and two children, by Israel. Copright A. R. Norton, 2000.

About 10 percent of all Muslims in the world are Shiᶜa. Both Shᶜia and the majority Sunni Muslims believe that the prophet Muhammad is the "Rasul," the Messenger of Allah, chosen by God to transmit His Word, and both accord special, central reverence to his memory, deeds, and actions as the last and most important prophet.

Although several doctrinal and legal issues separate the minority Shiᶜa from the Sunni majority, the most serious split is over the succession after the death of Prophet Muhammad, in 632 c.e. (10 a.h.). Only ᶜAli, the fourth and last of the four Rashidun—the "rightly guided" successors or Caliphs—is considered to have been a legitimate heir to the prophet by both the Shiᶜa and the Sunnis. Caliph ᶜAli, the son-in-law and cousin of Muhammad, served four years until his assassination in 660 c.e., in Kufa, a city in modern-day Iraq.

ᶜAli's death in Kufa, although mourned, has not made the deepest mark on Shiᶜism. The event that most shaped the ethos of Shiᶜa is called ᶜAshura, which refers to the fate of the grandson of the prophet Imam Hussein. Since the Shiᶜa believe that the successor should derive from the House of the Prophet, the sons of ᶜAli and his wife, the Prophet's daughter Fatimah, were favored. Two sons, Hasan and Hussein, are accepted by all Shiᶜa as leaders or Imams of the Muslim community. (A third son of ᶜAli by a different mother, ᶜAbbas, is a figure of military prowess and valor in Shiᶜi history and, as we shall see, has a leading role in Shiᶜa remembrance of that era.)

Imam Hussein is a central and beloved figure in the Shiᶜi imagination as an exemplar of courage, self-sacrifice, and compassion. When called by the people of Kufa in 680 c.e. (61 a.h.) to become their leader, Imam Hussein accepted the invitation and described his journey from Mecca as a mission to "restore my grandfather's community of Muslims." His decision to go to Kufa provoked a response from his adversary in Damascus, the ʿUmmayad Caliph Yazid, whose father Muʿawiyya succeeded Caliph ʿAli, Hussein's father, as the putative ruler of all Muslims.

The lessons of religion are captured in the dramas and tragedies of its heroes. In the case of the Shiʿa, the main event in their history is the story of Hussein's defeat and martyrdom, in 680 c.e., at the hands of Yazid's massive army at Karbala, in what is now modern Iraq. Surrounded, outmanned, yet refusing to submit to Yazid's authority, and thereby surrender his claim to be the successor to the prophet Muhammad, Imam Hussein's fate was sealed in a bloody confrontation lasting ten days on a blistering Iraqi plain. Hussein's martyrdom came on the tenth day of the first month of the Muslim calendar, Muharram—hence the use of the term ʿAshura, derived from the Arabic word for "tenth," to commemorate the event. The ʿAshura commemoration is shared by Shiʿi Muslims around the world—in Afghanistan, Bahrain, Iran, India, Indonesia, Iraq, Kuwait, Lebanon, Pakistan, Saudi Arabia, Syria, Turkey, Europe, and North America, as well as in smaller communities in the Gulf, and the Caribbean. ʿAshura is a time for reflection, worship, and mourning, and therefore weddings and other joyous events are not held during this period.

Hussein's sacrifice has special significance in recent history, as its reinterpretation by Musa al-Sadr, Ruhollah Khomeini, ʿAli Shariati, and other leading figures of Shiʿism provided the revolutionary exemplar for both the overthrow of the shah in Iran and the mobilization of Shiʿi Muslims in Lebanon. Hussein's martyrdom is presented as a model of courage, assertiveness, and self-help, and the modern interpretation of that event led to conclusions very similar to those arrived at by Catholic liberation theology: that people must not wallow in fatalism but must act to help themselves.

The detailed discussion in this chapter of the commemoration in Lebanon of Hussein's martyrdom provides a glimpse of a central aspect of Lebanese Shi'i society, as well as an appreciation of Hezbollah's largely successful efforts to shape Shi'a sensibilities for its own ends.

Ritual and Identity

Lebanon is a small country, roughly the size of Connecticut, but the venerable southern city of al-Nabatiya seems a continent away from the fussy lifestyles and bustling restaurants and cafes of cosmopolitan Beirut. The approximately sixty-minute drive from Beirut to Nabatiya is not just a departure from the capital's sensual delights but a sojourn to a part of the country that has lived in the vortex of conflict for more than three decades. Many Beiruti bon vivants are aghast at the prospect of making the southward trek.

Nabatiya is a commercial center in Jabal 'Amil, the Shi'i heartland that extends from the *wadis*[1] and hills of southern Lebanon to the southern Beqaa valley. Almost every weekend features a tidal flow of people from the overwhelmingly Shi'i Muslim suburbs of Beirut southward as Shi'a head to al-dai'ah ("the hamlet"), which is usually taken to mean "going to the countryside," where life is simple, wholesome, and unblemished by urban vices. Except in the bone-chilling, often icy winter in Jabal 'Amil, when people stay in Beirut and its environs, hundreds of thousands of people move back and forth weekly. Unfortunately, from the 1960s through 2006 the flow often reversed as the people of the

---

[1] A *wadi* is a dry streambed that swells with winter and spring rains and often becomes lush with vegetation until it dries up in the parching heat of summer.

Chapter 3

South sought refuge from bombardment and conflict with relatives in the comparative safety of the city.

Although the precise emergence of Shiᶜism in Jabal ᶜAmil is in dispute, the community unquestionably predates the introduction of Shiᶜism to Persia (Iran) in the sixteenth century. Certainly Jabal ᶜAmil was a center for scholarship as early as the late fourteenth century, and scholars from Jabal ᶜAmil (as well as from Iraq and Bahrain) assisted in the installation of Shiᶜi Islam in Safavid Persia. This was long before the Persian cities of Mashad or Qum became major centers of Shiᶜi scholarship. Jabal ᶜAmil continues to be revered by Shiᶜa, although it has long been eclipsed by al-Najaf and Karbala in Iraq, the two great Iraqi shrine cities, and, since the nineteenth century, by the now famous Iranian cities of Shiᶜi learning.

In Beirut, where members of Lebanon's eighteen recognized sects work and often live cheek to jowl, religious practice and ritual are often tucked away from public view (for a list of all the sects, see chapter 1, note 1). Lebanese are adept at discerning cues and clues that reveal an interlocutor's confessional roots and cultural identity, but, at least until recent decades, public religious ritual was often spurned to avoid provoking sectarian tension. Although public and private mourning of Imam Hussein (ᶜazah al-Hussein) and the tragic events (masaaᶜib) of Karbala, have long been observed in Shiᶜi communities, public commemorations of ᶜAshura are relatively recent phenomena in al-dahiya (literally "the suburb," the usual term for the densely populated southern suburbs of Beirut), where they began less than fifty years ago.

The practice of publicly mourning Imam Hussein (ᶜAshura) was introduced to the Beirut suburbs by a migrant from Baalbek, al-Hajj Ahmed al-Khansa, after he made pilgrimages (*ziyyarat*; literally, "visits"; singular, *ziyyara*), in 1938, to al-Najaf and Karbala, where he witnessed a number of public ceremonies during Muharram. On returning to Beirut, he instituted public mourning not simply as a display of communal piety but as a vehicle for mobilizing recent migrants to the city. Not surprisingly longtime residents and well-established Shiᶜa resisted ostentatious commemorations of ᶜAshura, which, they feared, might alienate their Christian neighbors who then controlled these areas politically (Khuri 1975). Hajj Ahmed built such a powerful foundation among the new urban residents that he eventually became a leading local politician.

In recent years, major public commemorations of ᶜAshura today take place in several parts of Lebanon, including *al-dahiyya*; in the Beqaa valley, especially in the city of Baalbek; the southern coastal city of Tyre; and across Jabal ᶜAmil. As many as a quarter of a million people either participate in or watch the military-style ᶜAshura parades organized by Hezbollah in the *al-dahiyya*. Much smaller, less tightly organized processions are held in Baalbek and in Tyre, with representation from various political and social organizations. Small-scale processions are conducted in villages and timed to precede larger commemorations in nearby towns and cities.

The most sensational commemorations are in Nabatiya, an overwhelmingly Shiᶜi city of thirty thousand people, where the event has a unique character. Public ᶜAshura rituals had been repressed by the Ottomans until their defeat in 1918, but annual mourning processions became popular in the 1920s and featured auto-flagellation and ritualized bleeding to mark the culmination of the Karbala tragedy.

Although the rituals of ᶜAshura commemoration are often debated vigorously among Shiᶜi, with religious leaders continually attempting to prescribe "appropriate" ways of remembering ʿAshura, local practices vary widely and popular local customs blend in with Islamic traditions.

Among the Shiʿa, commemorative ritual processions sometimes include flailing oneself with chains, metal whips, or swords or intentionally nicking the skin on the forehead to induce bleeding (*tatbir*), as well as the more common practice of rhythmically beating one's chest with a balled fist (*latam*). Of course, this is not to every Shiʿi's taste, and some prefer quiet contemplation and prayer to public performance. Clerical disapproval has been strong; like many of his colleagues, the popular and respected (and al-Najaf born) Ayatollah Muhammad Hussein Fadlallah argues that the blood rituals of Nabatiya are improper pragmatically, as they put Shiʿi Muslims in a bad light in the eyes of non-Shiʿa, but they also violate religious law that does not allow Muslims to injure or kill themselves. He emphasizes that the self-flagellation and similar rituals are "socially backward," even "reactionary." Instead, the events of Muharram must be understood as a model for an intellectual revolution. Similarly the Ayatollah Muhammad Mahdi Shams al-Din, who until his death in 2001 was one of the most respected clerical voices among the Shiʿa, urged that Imam Hussein's sacrifice be understood ethically and normatively, not simply as an occasion for demonstrative tears or sensational rituals (Shams al-Din 1985). Along similar lines, the Iranian leader ʿAli Khamenei issued a 1994 *fatwa* (an authoritative religious opinion; pl., *futawa*) condemning the shedding of blood during Muharram rituals and underlining the negative image the rituals project. He argued that these rituals were not Islamic but the product of tradition. (Hezbollah has embraced Khamenei as the supreme Shiʿi leader and has promoted his views.) Virtually every important Shiʿi cleric, with few exceptions, has condemned and forbidden the practice in recent years and issued *futawa* calling on Shiʿa not to participate.

Still, predominantly male rituals of bloodletting of various sorts have proven remarkably resilient in the face of persistent clerical disapproval. Bleeding is an important aspect of the ritual for many—but by no means all—of the participants in Shiʿi commemorations of ʿAshura in Nabatiya (although it is practiced in Shiʿi communities in India, Iran, Iraq, and Pakistan, it is uncommon elsewhere in Lebanon). As one articulate enthusiast, an optometrist in Nabatiya, told me as we watched the spectacle in 2000, "What you see here is the real Islam. Islam is not found in books, it is here [in the ritual]." In addition to the label *tatbir*, the ritual is sometimes locally called *haidar*, meaning lion, a reference to Hussein's father Imam ʿAli, the son-in-law of the prophet who is revered for his wisdom. As men run through the streets, they sometimes simply chant "*haidar, haidar, haidar*," as they strike their foreheads with the open palm of their hands or occasionally with a blade.

From the first day of Muharram, black banners are draped on buildings and hung across the streets of Nabatiya, as they are throughout the Shiʿi areas of Lebanon. (In contrast, when the author visited Tehran during ʿAshura 2004 such public signage was much less common). The banners proclaim: "Everyone is calling for Hussein"; "Every day is ʿAshura and every land is Karbala"; "Crying for Hussein is a victory of the oppressed over the oppressor"; or a variety of similar messages. Black pennants are fastened to power and light poles invoking "Hussein," "the Awaited One," "ʿAbbas," or "Haidar."

During Muharram, entrepreneurs open roadside stands and impromptu ʿAshura souvenir shops to sell tapes and books of readings from the saga of ʿAshura and the killing (*al-maqtal*) of Hussein, as well as cassettes of mourning lamentations, buttons, banners, paperweights, posters, and other keepsakes. A variety of clothing is offered, including T-shirts for youngsters and adults, and baseball caps with ᶜAshura slogans. Many of these ᶜAshura mementos are manufactured in Iran and imported by enterprising Lebanese traders attracted by Iran's bargain basement prices. Shiᶜi men and women dress in subdued clothing, and many men wear black trousers and shirts to mark this period of ritual mourning. In addition, the two rival political organizations compete, handing out an array of scarves, vests, head and wristbands, caps, and pennants, all emblazoned with the logos of Amal or Hezbollah in distinctive color combinations (green, red, and white for Amal; black, red, and especially yellow for Hezbollah).

For the first ten days of the Muharram, daily readings in private homes and in Husseiniyas (centers for the observance of Hussein's martyrdom) recall the drama and tragedy of Karbala (*masaaᶜib*; sing., *masaba*). The usual pattern in many villages and neighborhoods is to hold readings in one's home or with neighbors, followed by an evening visit to the Husseiniya. (There are sometimes separate Husseiniyas for men and women; if not, women retreat to a separate section of the men's Husseiniya). In these gatherings (*majalis*), skilled readers are often hired to relate the *masaaᶜib* and recite *al-taᶜziya*, the lamentations of mourning, which are also read in contemporary Lebanon to mourn the death of a loved one. The fate of Hussein and his followers is, of course, well known: all the men and boys will die, save Hussein's infant son ᶜAli Zayn al-ᶜAbdin, who will carry on the Imamate as the successor to the Prophet Muhammad, and the surviving women will suffer horrible humiliation and suffering at the hand of Yazid, Hussein's triumphant rivals. Listen-

ers often respond with tears, and crying is *mustahhab* or com-
mendable. A variety of Shi⁗i sources include the succeeding
Imams' emphasis that the weeping for Hussein and his family is rewarded in the hereafter, and that tears (and prayers)
offered in this context will be rewarded at the Day of Judgment (Ayoub 1978). Readings often continue throughout
the month, focusing especially on the tribulations of the
women captives.

Zainab, Hussein's sister, is honored and discussed as a
strong figure, an exemplar for women. Her endurance of suffering and her courage to speak truth to power when she
was brought in captivity to the court of Yazid in Damascus is
now understood as an archetype for women. Women usually
gather separately from men in private homes or, as noted
above, in a separate Husseiniya.

In one prosperous village, just outside Nabatiya, a lovely
women's Husseiniya was built a decade ago by a wealthy
resident who shared the consensus of the community that a
women's Husseiniya was the most important community
need. The author asked a female doctor from Beirut, "Had
there always been a women's Husseiniya in the village?" She
answered yes, but it used to be [switching to English]
'shitty.'" Her comment illustrates the transformation in recent years among Lebanese Shi⁗i women, who now are
much less inclined than in the past to derive a counsel of
despair from ⁗Ashura. Just as the larger meaning of ⁗Ashura
has changed in recent decades to encompass more activist
interpretations, so Zainab's exemplar provides encourage-
ment for Shi⁗i women to move decisively and courageously
in society (Deeb 2006).

In contrast to other sites in Lebanon, the processions in
Nabatiya last for two full days, encompassing both the ninth
and tenth days of Muharram. Nabatiya's population swells

in Muharram as Shiʿa from Nabatiya and southern Lebanon, and even from abroad, close in on the city to mark the event. Wealthy Shiʿa who work abroad often bring their friends and relatives. Hajj Majid Rihan, a rich son of Nabatiya who lives and works in Gabon, flew co-religionists, in 2000, from West Africa to Lebanon on a charter jet to take part in the rituals. Accurate crowd counts are always a challenge, but local authorities estimate that as many as fifty thousand people crowd into the city annually. Most participants have been Lebanese, but in recent years contingents of Shiʿa have arrived from Iraq and Iran, though few Iranians have participated recently.

On the ninth and tenth days of Muharram, many hundreds of men, boys, and even infants, as well as a handful of young women, embrace the suffering of Imam Hussein by shedding their blood in memory of his martyrdom. Since the 1990s several public health organizations, as well as Hezbollah, have called upon people to make blood donations rather than inflict bleeding upon themselves, and a blood collection station enjoyed a steady clientele. It is not uncommon for *darribeen* (those who strike themselves) to bleed ritually and also donate blood, and even female workers at the blood donor station sometimes join the ritual.

The Intersection of Ritual and Politics

ʿAshura is not merely the grass-roots practice of religion. It is also a political event, an opportunity for the rival Amal movement and Hezbollah to show their strength and demonstrate their solidarity. When the author observed the event in March 2000, just two months before the Israeli withdrawal from the "security zone," enthusiastic Amal sup-

3.1 Members of the Amal movement participating in the bleeding ritual, which is a popular religious ritual in southern Lebanon, and one that is condemned by many clerics and dismissed as a folk ritual by Hezbollah. Copyright A. R. Norton, 2000.

porters, many from southern Lebanese villages, were every-where in evidence, but Hezbollah also enjoyed a strong core of support in the town, which was reinforced four years later when the party triumphed in municipal elections in Nabat-iya (more on this in chapter 5). In 2000 both groups were well represented in the parades or processions on both days, and thousands of others were spectators. Whereas the Amal marchers seemed to be loosely organized but not unruly, Hezbollah members marched with military precision and or-ganized effective cordons for crowd control. The contrast between the loosely organized, populist Amal and the tightly disciplined Hezbollah was quite obvious. Both groups marshaled men, women, and children for their processions, and the numerous children were organized by age or school grade, although the Hezbollah groups were by far more regi-

3.2 In this part of the dramatic reenactment of the events of Karbala in 680 ce, Hussein's half-brother ʿAbbas, a famous warrior clad here in white, is fighting the enemy. Copyright A. R. Norton, 2000.

mented. Even women with babies in their arms, or pushing baby strollers, were enlisted to march.

The Lebanese army and police are usually much in evidence, and sometimes confrontations erupt with a political flavor. At one point, in 2000, the army fired a few shots in the air to disperse some shoving matches between participants, whose adrenaline had gotten the better of their good judgment. The same year a van carrying men from a pro-Amal village was turned away from the entrance to Nabatiya, when soldiers discovered that the men were armed; an altercation followed in which an army officer was punched, but the soldiers prevailed.

More serious clashes occurred in 2002, when sixty people were injured and dozens of cars damaged in melees involving angry Amal and Hezbollah members. The Amalists charged that the Hezbollah parade ran overtime and delayed their own processions (*masirat*) by an hour. Hezbollah boycotted

Nabatiya in 2003, and its television channel, al-Manar, did not cover the *tatbir* ritual the next year.

Notwithstanding the clashes between rival hotheads, the mood is usually friendly and welcoming. The public commemoration actually occupies two days, in contrast to all the other Shiʿi locales in Lebanon. On *al-tasuʿa*—the ninth day of Muharram—there are dozens of processions of *darribeen* as people begin to gather in al-Nabatiya. Despite the heavy stench of blood, particularly on al-ʿAshura—the tenth day—visitors often remark on a carnival-like atmosphere. After participating in the processions, *shabaab*, or young men, casually walk the street showing off their blood-splattered clothes as testimony to their fidelity to Shiʿism and to their bravado. Teenaged girls enjoy themselves, sometimes ogling their male contemporaries and, of course, giggling. A handful of young women participate in the bloodletting, but they usually number no more than a few dozen at most. Street vendors sell snacks and drinks, but many people purchase cases of juice and water which they dispense to anyone wishing to quench his or her thirst. Local restaurant owners cook dozens of sheep that they donate to feed hundreds of people.

Perhaps most important, ʿAshura is a family holiday and an occasion for reunions and feasts. It is also the occasion for special foods, and some of the faithful work late into the night preparing tens of kilos of food for free distribution. Women spend days preparing particular foods associated with ʿAshura. The most common is *harisa*, which is made by soaking and softening wheat overnight and then cooking it three or four hours before adding shredded chicken to the pudding-like product. The *harisa* is seasoned with cinnamon and cloves, and then offered to family and visitors or even passersby. In other Arab countries, such as Iraq, *harisa* is

3.3 Four young women from southern Lebanon enjoying the holiday spectacle of al-Ashura in al-Nabatiya. Copyright A. R. Norton, 2000.

sweetened. *Qima*, a less commonly prepared dish from al-Najaf in Iraq, features chick peas, tomatoes, and cooked red meat which some see as symbolizing the blood sacrifice of Hussein and his followers.

Participating in the bleeding ritual is an individual choice, although the parents of many young boys clearly encourage them to take part. Many of the participants start out at the Husseiniya, where a heaving crowd of thousands gather. Using a straight razor, or *mouss*, and deft flicks of the wrist, an obliging barber inflicts shallow cuts on the upper forehead. One or two suffices to cause some bleeding, but some participants wish to bleed more demonstrably and so they will have five, ten, or even more cuts made or do it themselves. (Health-conscious, middle-class *darribeen* bring their own razors, which can be purchased inexpensively for about a dollar.) Participants then join a group and follow a prescribed route past the *bidar*, or field, where the ʿAshura events are dramatized, and then around the main streets of the town, culminating at the Husseiniya.

"Everyone has their own Hussein," notes Ali Safa, a respected professor in Beirut whose natal village is nearby. Some people have participated in the ritual all their lives and cannot imagine missing it. Others do so to fulfill a *nithir*, or pledge. Ra'ed Moukalled is a local optometrist who lost a son, Ahmad, in 1999, during a picnic the day before his fifth birthday; the boy had picked up what looked like a toy but was an unexploded cluster bomb dropped by Israel. Ra'id participates in the ritual annually in tribute to his deceased son, and his friends join him to show their support and to share in his personal tragedy. Ra'id has also been a civic leader actively involved in efforts to work with international nongovernmental organizations (NGOs) to clear cluster bombs and mines from southern Lebanon. Even a few Christians get involved in the Hussein ritual, either out of community spirit or to fulfill their own pledge, perhaps to mark the recovery of an ill relative or a reversal of family fortunes.

The mood of the bloodletting rituals is infectious and often onlookers impulsively join the bloodletting. This author has seen a couple of Lebanese policemen and soldiers do just that, slipping on a civilian shirt and returning to don their uniform with a blood-stained bandage secure on their forehead. Aid stations do a robust business, applying bandages and reviving those who have fainted from heat exhaustion or loss of blood. In winter or early spring the weather is usually comfortable, but when ʿAshura falls in the hot months of summer the heat and dehydration claim many more casualties. Nonetheless, no deaths from the ritual have been reported.

3.4 Hezbollah members participating in an ʿAshura procession in southern Lebanon. Posters depict ʿAbbas al-Musawi (in the foreground) the Hezbollah leader assassinated by Israel in 1992, and Musa al-Sadr, the Iranian of Lebanese descent who founded the Shiʿi movement in Lebanon. Copyright A. R. Norton, 2000.

The dramatization of ʿAshura, the *timthilyya* (a play or performance), takes place on a *bidar*, or field, in front of the city's large Husseiniya. The rendition of the *timthiliyya* often lasts more than three hours. Thousands of people crowd around the field or on the roofs of neighboring buildings to watch the event. In 2000 Yazid's soldiers wore lurid florescent costumes in yellow and orange, whereas Hussein's somber troupe decamped at a green-rimmed tent, after entering the field on camels and parading before the crowd. A large Islamic standard waves to mark the camp of the prophet's grandson. A narrator reads a script, but the players themselves, Hussein as well, often recite their lines, much to the displeasure of some clerics. One such cleric, Shaikh Qabalan, disapproves of the entire play, strongly objecting to the idea that any person could portray Hussein.

Historically, on the seventh day of Muharram, Hussein's group was cut off from water, and heroic battles were fought to reach the Euphrates River, in this reenactment a small concrete pond. As the replay of history continues, Hussein's half-brother, ʿAbbas, a brilliant warrior and Hussein's standard-bearer, succeeds in reaching the water twice. The first time, never taking a sip himself, he watches helplessly as the hard-won water spills onto the sand, and thirsty and anxious children attempt to open the leather water bag. The second time he fails to return. ʿAbbas fights fiercely, and is only defeated when both his hands are severed at the wrists. The *kaff* ʿAbbas, literally the palms of ʿAbbas, are a central motif in parade floats and displays throughout the day.

The drama takes it toll on the crowd, a number of women faint, exhausted by the emotion-wrenching play and fatigued from standing in place for hours. At particularly poignant moments, such as the death of Hussein's son, Ali al-Akbar, who is said to have resembled his great-grandfather Muhammad, women are sobbing loudly. The death of an infant in Hussein's arms evokes a similar chorus of sobs. The play is punctuated by long soliloquies from Hussein and by his entreaties to the enemy. He offers to withdraw from Karbala but refuses to pay homage to Yazid; hence his fate is cast. Imam Hussein reflects on injustice, on the price of loyalty to Islam, on the need to confront our own death bravely, to sacrifice our own flesh and blood in order to see Allah. He is the last man to die, slain while badly wounded and in prayer. His severed head is carried to Damascus in tribute to Yazid, and his body is trampled along with the corpses of his followers by the enemy horsemen. The women of his band are marched off into misery. Variants of the *timthilyya* are performed annually, and lessons of the tragedy are not lost on the rapt audience.

Chapter 3

In 1983, just as the drama was being performed and groups
of blood-splattered celebrants were milling about in front
of the Husseiniya, an armed Israeli patrol of several trucks
suddenly appeared and attempted to crash through the
crowds. The incident was caused when an Israeli lieutenant,
who had been ordered to avoid the town on ʿAshura, misread his map and took the wrong road. The scene is easy
enough to imagine, as the occupiers were instantly seen in
the role of Yazid. The crowd threw stones and the Israelis
responded with rifles and grenades, killing several Shiʿa.
The incident was a turning point in the resistance to Israel's
occupation, especially as it spurred many previous fence-
sitters to join the resistance. In Lebanon's Shiʿi community
the 1983 incident is intrinsic to a commonly shared narra-
tive emphasizing Israel's disrespect for Islam and the injustice of the long Israeli occupation.

Another event still talked about is the 1996 massacre in
Qana, the southern Lebanese town where more than a hundred people were killed in the Israeli shelling of the UNIFIL
base in Qana (more on this in chapter 4). Floats in the Muharram parade often recall the massacre, emphasizing anti-
Israel themes and memorializing the resistance. Individuals
frequently make the same connection that was so easily
made by the crowds in 1983, that the Israeli occupiers are
the modern incarnation of Yazid. In contrast to the tragedy
that befell Hussein, however, this time the Shiʿa, having
learned from Karbala, will confront and defeat Yazid.

Until recent decades the rituals of Muharram in Lebanon
had reified and affirmed the status quo, and taught quiescence. Half a century ago the renowned anthropologist
Emyrs Peters studied a Shiʿi village in Jabal ʿAmil, where
he found that the play, the *timthilyya*, was a conservative
device for sustaining an existing order, not challenging it.

What the Play did was to give the vast audience a glimpse of the kind of world they could anticipate when evil triumphs. What was depicted was a world of madness, a world of complete unreason, a world without order of any sort. It did not depict a revolutionary situation of one group supplanting another—indeed, the peasantry could never supplant the Learned Families in this sense, for the peasants are far too numerous. What it showed was the chaos that would result if the Learned Families lost their control of village affairs. (Peters 1970)

Contemporary ʿAshura rituals, however, exemplify, and indeed encourage, a heightened and widespread sense of politicization. The ceremonies are an occasion for competing political organizations to perform contending variations of the ritual in order to exemplify piety and mobilize support. In this sense, the rituals offer no less than a public performance of ideology, with, for example, rituals explicitly casting Israel in the role of Caliph Yazid, the ʿUmmayad ruler responsible for Imam Hussein's martyrdom. Lebanese politicians in the Amal and Hezbollah organizations work hard to harness these sentiments to their advantage, often with impressive success. A striking illustration of this in recent years is the televised addresses by Hezbollah's current secretary-general al-Sayyid Hasan Nasrallah during the first ten days of Muharram, which are viewed attentively by multitudes. Nasrallah is a popular and often riveting speaker, and his nightly Muharram sermons often probe the "real meaning" of ʿAshura, analyzing why death is not to be feared and offering an explicit political commentary. His sermons routinely have two parts, one more or less religious and the other political, in which he routinely castigates the United States for its policies in the Middle East and sometimes comments more generally on U.S. affairs. In February 2005 he emphasized the inherent justice of Hezbollah's cause, inspired as it was by the Imam Hussein's quest, and he railed against depictions of the party as a "terrorist" group. At other times the talks during the month of Muharram are used to offer a social critique, as in March 2000, when one of Nasrallah's sermons scathingly assessed America's social ills, underlining that nation's social problems in order to dampen the dreams of many Shiʿa to immigrate to America.

Prior to Israel's May 2000 unilateral withdrawal of its occupation forces from southern Lebanon, Nasrallah's Muharram sermons were major political statements, listened to carefully by a wide audience of apprehensive Lebanese for hints about whether chaos or order would follow Israel's impending withdrawal. He astutely anticipated that there would be little disorder. Whatever one thinks about his views, Nasrallah also exploited the occasion of Muharram to further legitimate Hezbollah as a social and political force among the Shiʿa. The party benefited from a wave of support for its leading role in fighting Israel and creating the pressure that prompted Israel's withdrawal. In contrast to Lebanon's elected political leaders, who seemed thoroughly flummoxed by Israel's declared intention to leave southern Lebanon, with or without an agreement with Syria, Nasrallah projected a tough, clearheaded image.

Chapter 4
Resistance, Terrorism, and Violence in Lebanon

Two Shiʿi participants in ʿAshura processions in Nabatiya. Both wear headbands honoring the Imam Hussein as the leader of martyrs. Copyright A. R. Norton, 2000.

The 1980s was a decade of extraordinary violence and chaos in Lebanon, often remembered in the United States with indelible images of the ruins of the U.S. marine barracks obliterated by a suicide bomber on a Sunday morning in October 1983. The lives of 220 marines, 18 sailors, and 3 soldiers, in addition to the wife and four children of a Lebanese janitor, were snuffed out in the attack. Simultaneously 58 French paratroopers were killed by a second bomb-laden truck. The French, like the Americans, were participants in the Multinational Force (MNF) that had been dispatched to Beirut to bring stability to Lebanon in the wake of the June 1982 Israeli invasion of that country. Israel's goals were twofold: to destroy the PLO as an important political force and to install a friendly government in Beirut. The MNF's involvement began that summer after the retreat of most armed Palestinian guerrillas from Lebanon by ship and land. More than three hundred thousand Palestinians remained, most of them refugees or descendents of refugees from the first Palestinian war of 1948–49. After the catastrophic suicide bombings of October 1983, the marines, to use Ronald Reagan's word, "redeployed" by early 1984, and the MNF ceased to exist.

There is little question that the attacks were carried out by Lebanese Shi'i militants, under Iranian direction. A blue-ribbon investigating commission established by the American government and headed by retired admiral Robert L. J. Long, described the October bombing as an "act of war" and found Iran largely responsible. Iran is also widely believed to be responsible for the earlier suicide bombing and decimation of the U.S. Embassy in Beirut in April 1983. The oft-unnoticed precedent for the 2003 attacks was established in mid-December 1981, when the Iraqi Embassy in Beirut was leveled by a suicide bomber. The Iraqi al-Da'wa party claimed credit for the attack, citing Iraq's invasion of Iran in September 1980.

Lebanon, porous to outside influence and militarily weak, had long been the site for proxy wars, and this was especially the case in the 1980s, with war materials supplied by rival political and military sponsors, including Iraq, Iran, Syria, Libya, Israel, the United States, France, Saudi Arabia, and the Soviet Union. Among the contestants for power, Syria and Iran played key roles, though not always in cooperation with each other. Although Damascus and Teheran shared an interest in thwarting U.S. influence in Lebanon and defeating Israel's occupation of the country, throughout the decade Syria revealed great suspicion of Iran and its protégé, Hezbollah. Early in the 1980s Hezbollah existed less as a concrete organization than as a cat's paw of Iran. As Hezbollah's strength grew over the course of the decade, Syria periodically tried to contain it, most dramatically when the al-Asad regime killed twenty-three Hezbollah members in 1987. Syria also provided support to Amal in that rival Shiʿa organization's ferocious battles with Hezbollah, in 1988 and 1989. Four years earlier, in 1985, Syria also provided material support for Amal's "war of the camps," a three-year campaign to eliminate the power base of Palestinian militants in the refugee camps surrounding Beirut. Although Amal imposed great suffering on Palestinians in the camps, the armed Palestinian militants were never fully subdued, largely because Hezbollah gave them extensive support. Whereas many Amal members were hostile to the Palestinian guerrillas for their abusive behavior in southern Lebanon, Hezbollah supported them on principle. The revered Shiʿa religious authority Ayatollah Muhammad Hussein Fadlallah backed Hezbollah's position and condemned the Amal campaign. Because of this crucial clerical approval, and despite Syrian opposition, Hezbollah won increasing support among the local Shi'a. By 1990 the organization had largely supplanted Amal in the environs of Beirut.

Lebanon became infamous, in the 1980s, for the kidnapping of Westerners, thirty in all, most of whom were hapless innocents snared at a time of venomous xenophobia. Kidnapping for vengeance, politics, or profit was a well-practiced craft throughout the civil war. After the Israeli invasion in June 1982, however, the first foreigners kidnapped were not Westerners but four Iranian diplomats snatched by the Maronite Lebanese Forces militia and subsequently murdered. The string of Western hostages began in 1982 with David Dodge, the president of the American University of Beirut (AUB), who was held for a year, including some time in Iran. The Dodge kidnapping was apparently intended as a rejoinder to the disappearance of the four Iranians, as well as to strike a blow at the most obvious and well-known symbol of America's connection to Lebanon, namely, the AUB.

There was no "kidnapping-central" but a cabal of militants, some certainly linked to Hezbollah, others in various other gangs and groups, including some that were in the hostage business, selling and trading hostages for profit (a phenomenon that presaged similar criminal activities in Iraq). The UN official who played the lead role in many of the hostage negotiations was Giandominico Picco, whose memoir, Man without a Gun (Random House, 1999), leaves little doubt that Syria had almost no influence over the kidnappers, and Iran's leverage was operationally limited.

Although Iran did not exercise direct control of the kidnappings, its revolutionary regime did exert strong ideological influence and was particularly effective at sowing the suspicion that Westerners in Lebanon were agents for imperialist Americans and Israelis. The hostage seizures were fully consistent with Hezbollah's declared goal of expunging America from Lebanon, its citizens as well as its diplomatic presence. Western hostages were held in Lebanon in despicable conditions, often alone and chained to radiators for months on end, denied even the slightest dignity. The longest held was Terry Anderson, a reporter for the Associated Press, who spent seven long years as a hostage. CIA Station Chief William Buckley died in captivity, after being brutally interrogated and tortured. The hostages' fate was often manipulated to serve the interests of Hezbollah's sponsor, Iran. Lebanon became so dangerous for Americans that, in 1987, the State Department banned the use of U.S. passports for travel to the country, a ban that was not lifted until 1997 (although tens of thousands of Americans ignored the ban in the 1990s after the civil war ended and simply avoided having their passports stamped).

The hostage crisis gave rise to "Iran-Contra," the 1986 scandal that revealed the willingness of then U.S. president Ronald Reagan to trade arms to Iran in return for the freeing of hostages. Unfortunately the hostage releases made possible by these deals were shortly followed by the snatching of others, and four more years would pass before the hostage era ended in Lebanon. Unquestionably Iran exploited the hostages to serve its interests. Deputy Minister of Foreign Affairs Hosein Sheikholeslam confirmed Iran's stake, when, in 1988, he expressed his hope that "the hostage situation would be resolved in a way that serves the objectives for which they were kidnapped." (Chehabi 1988, 228)

Lebanon was a cockpit for violence and a breeding ground for terrorism in the 1980s, but endemic violence began to ebb as the civil war ended in 1989 and 1990. Simultaneously Syria tightened its control over Lebanon with the implicit

consent of the U.S., which rewarded Syria's symbolic participation in the 1990–91 Gulf War coalition against Iraq's
invasion of Kuwait. In the South, however, Israel's occupation continued to provoke resistance, not least by Hezbollah. Before turning to a fuller examination of the situation
in southern Lebanon in the course of the 1990s, we should
pause to reflect more generally on the relationship between
terrorism and political violence.

Hezbollah and Terrorism

Can all of Hezbollah's military activity be classified as terrorism? U.S. and Israeli policymakers certainly think so, and
they have defined Hezbollah as a terrorist organization.
Anyone supporting Hezbollah is supporting a terrorist
group. By definition, any act of violence that it commits or
seeks to commit is an act of terrorism, and so there are no
gray areas of justifiable behavior in which terrorists may
lurk. Whether for law enforcement officials, spies, or soldiers, the issue is assumed to be settled.

"Terrorist" is a useful rhetorical bludgeon that many states
have wielded to outlaw or de-humanize radical or revolutionary groups. Thus, throughout the 1970s and 1980s, before Israel and the Palestine Liberation Organization signed
the Oslo accords, almost any mention of PLO included the
description "terrorist," and any Israeli aerial bombing of the
PLO, which was in those days a major armed presence in
Lebanon, was an attack on terrorist targets, according to
Israeli spokespersons and journalists.

Following the attacks on New York City and the Penta-
gon by al-Qaeda on September 11, 2001, President George
W. Bush signed Executive Order 13224 specifying a series
of steps that were to taken to combat al-Qaeda, and its affil-

iates and resources. The groups described in that executive order as terrorists of "global reach" did not include Hezbollah, even though the U.S. Department of State, in 1997, had labeled it a "foreign terrorist organization." Nor was the Palestinian Islamist group Hamas included, even though it, too, had long been included in the State Department's terrorist list.

These omissions prompted a lively debate, with pro-Israeli lobbying groups, particularly the American-Israel Public Affairs Committee, the influential Washington-based group that describes itself as "America's pro-Israel lobby," as well as a number of members of Congress, arguing strenuously for including Hezbollah and Hamas in the terms of the executive order. Many officials resisted the move, arguing that America's focus should be on al-Qaeda, the group responsible for the 9/11 attacks, and noting that the U.S. would need the support of many Arab states that recognize Hamas and Hezbollah as bona fide resistance groups. Although leading figures in the Bush administration, notably Secretary of Defense Donald Rumsfeld, maintained that the additional designation was unnecessary and redundant, the administration amended the executive order to include Hezbollah and other groups as enemies in the "war against terrorism." In Israel, the government of Prime Minister Ariel Sharon moved quickly in the days following 9/11 to associate Israel with America's war on terrorism, thereby gaining further leverage against Israel's enemies.

Terrorism can be defined as the intentional use of political violence against civilians and civilian sites such as schools, hospitals, restaurants, buses, trains, or planes. Putting aside for the moment that Hezbollah promotes activities and performs services in Lebanon that have nothing to do with terrorism, such as running hospitals, the organization has engaged in forms of violence that fall outside the rubric of terrorism as it is generally understood. Most notably, so long as Israel was occupying a significant area of Lebanon, there is no doubt that Hezbollah and other Lebanese groups were fully within their rights to resist the occupation forces and to do so with deadly violence. That the resistance usually restricted its attacks to enemy soldiers and the enemy's proxy forces only reinforced their firm normative footing. The primary reason why the United States has not succeeded in convincing most European states to endorse its blanket designation of Hezbollah as "terrorist" is because many of those states insist on a more precise conception of terrorism than the U.S. habitually employs. Of course, once Israel withdrew unilaterally from Lebanon, in 2000, Hezbollah found itself on far weaker normative ground.

Also, there is no question that Hezbollah has engaged in acts that do, indeed, constitute terrorism in its more precise and generally understood sense. One such clear instance was the 1985 skyjacking, by two Hezbollah operatives, of TWA flight 847, en route from Athens to Rome, Robert Stethem, a U.S. sailor on leave and traveling on the flight, was mercilessly beaten and shot in the head. The hijackers, Imad Mughniyah and Hasan Izz al-Din, who remain close to the top of the FBI's "wanted list," disgracefully dumped his body on the tarmac of Beirut airport. Another clear-cut case, cited previously in chapter 2, was the 1998 kidnapping of Lieutenant Colonel William R. Higgins of the U.S. Marines, an unarmed UN observer who was tortured and murdered by the "Believers' Resistance," a group sympathetic to Hezbollah.

It is generally easier to trace much of the terrorism of the 1980s and early 1990s to Iran than to Hezbollah. Iran murdered a variety of regime opponents during this time,

77

including Shapur Bakhtiar, the last prime minister of the Pahlavi dynasty that had been overthrown in 1979, as well as members of the Pahlavi family and other former officials of the toppled regime. Especially at risk were Kurdish nationalists, who advocated greater autonomy or independence for the Kurdish minority in Iran. After the killing of four Kurds in a Greek restaurant in Berlin, an Iranian intelligence official boasted that a blow had been struck at the Kurdish opposition. An Iranian official and three Lebanese were convicted in a 1997 trial of the Berlin assassinations, and four other Iranian officials who were judged responsible, in absentia, included President Rafsanjani and the Supreme Leader of Iran, Ali Khamenei. The evidence of Iranian complicity in many of these attacks is clear to any impartial observer. The extent of Hezbollah's involvement, however, is murkier. Robert Baer, a former CIA agent with extensive experience in Lebanon and in the Middle East, has argued that Hezbollah was not involved: "It's not that Hezbollah is doing the terrorism out of Lebanon. They didn't do the US Embassy in 1983 or the Marines. It was the Iranians. It's a political issue [in the U.S.] because the Israelis want the Americans to go after Hezbollah" (*Christian Science Monitor*, July 7, 2003). But although Baer's conclusions are accurate for many of the attacks in Europe during this period, in other instances Hezbollah's role is more clearly indicated. Following Israel's 1992 assassination of Hezbollah Secretary-General ʿAbbas Musawi, two terrorist attacks occurred in Argentina that many knowledgeable observers believe were the joint work of Iran and Hezbollah's external security organization, which apparently operates autonomously from the party and is widely believed to be closely linked to Iranian intelligence. The first attack, within months of Musawi's murder, was the detonation of a large bomb under the Israeli Embassy in Buenos Aries, killing twenty-nine people. The Argentinean authorities issued an arrest warrant for Hezbollah operative Imad Mughniyeh, one of the two hijackers of TWA flight 847 in 1985, a man believed to have regularly collaborated with Iran in acts of terrorism.

The second attack, in 1994, was the result of a bomb-laden van driven into the Buenos Aries–based Israeli association, killing eighty-five people, most of them Jews. The suicide bomber was allegedly Hezbollah member Ibrahim Hussein Berro, but Hezbollah claims that he died later in southern Lebanon in a resistance operation. The former Iranian ambassador to Argentina Hade Soleimanpour was later briefly arrested in Britain but was released for lack of evidence. Then, in November 2006, warrants were issued for the arrest of former Iranian president Akbar Hashemi Rafsanjani and eight other former Iranian officials including the ex-foreign minister Ali-Akbar Velayati.

Occupation in Southern Lebanon

Israel's occupation of southern Lebanon spanned more than two decades and rendered Hezbollah's ideology persuasive to many Shiʿa in the region. Israel's military involvement in the South began in 1978 with its "Litani Operation," intended to push Palestinian guerrillas north of the Litani River. The invasion left important pockets of armed Palestinian strength intact, but it provided a context for creating a border "security zone" under the nominal control of a proxy militia led initially by the volatile, renegade Lebanese army major Sa'ad Haddad. Despite the terms of UN Security Resolution 425, passed in 1978 with heavy U.S. support and calling for the withdrawal of Israeli forces and the restoration of Lebanese sovereignty, Israel sustained this security zone for the next twenty-two years until unilaterally withdrawing in 2000. By that time Hezbollah had, indisputably, become both Israel's nemesis and a central fixture among Shi'a in southern Lebanon.

Within months of Israel's June 1982 invasion, when it became clear that Israel had no intention of disengaging from Lebanon anytime soon, a variety of groups across the political spectrum began to organize attacks against the Israeli occupation forces. These included factions of the Ba'th and Communist parties, Nasserist organizations, and other secular nationalist groups. By the 1990s, however, Hezbollah was carrying out most of the attacks, each appearing to have been characterized by careful planning and well-practiced professionalism. Its first post-invasion operation, and one of its deadliest, was mounted in November 1982, in the southern city of Tyre. Hezbollah member Shaikh Ahmad Qasir drove a bomb-laden car into an Israeli headquarters and intelligence center. At least seventy-five Israeli officials and soldiers were killed, along with fourteen Arab prisoners. The attack was so unexpected that Israel did not even know initially how it had happened and for years persisted in saying that the explosion was caused by a "gas leakage."[1]

The Tyre attack, in fact, was one of twelve "self-martyrdom missions" (in Hezbollah parlance) mounted by Hezbollah members. This was less than one-third of all the suicide attacks. The other suicide missions were launched by Amal and various secular nationalist groups all intent on ending Israel's occupation. This distribution of suicide missions

---

[1] For an official Israeli report of the incident, see http://www.mfa.gov.il/ MFA/Foreign%20Relations/Israels%20Foreign%20Relations%20since%201947/ 1982-1984.

between secular and Islamist-leaning groups illustrates that the tactic of mounting suicide attacks was motivated more often by nationalist and patriotic impulses than by religious inspiration.

The turning point in the resistance was the 1983 Nabatiya incident described in the previous chapter, when an Israeli army patrol blundered into the middle of the town during a mass procession on ʿAshura and opened fire in an attempt to disperse the crowd. From that time on there would be no fence sitting. By 1984 the pace of attacks was so intense that an Israeli soldier was dying every third day.

In 1985 Israel hunkered down in an enlarged border zone comprising some 10 percent of all Lebanese territory which the Israelis referred to by the euphemism "security zone." Israel asserted that it would abide by UN Resolution 425, calling for unconditional Israeli withdrawal only after the security situation improved. In reality, this was an *in*security zone that became an argument for continuing occupation. If the situation in the South quieted, as it did periodically, Israeli officials held up the zone as a success that could not be safely terminated. When the situation became hotter, the zone became a necessity. Effectively the zone was an impetus to violence.

Hezbollah officials, meanwhile, frequently claimed that, without effective Shiʿi resistance to the occupation, Israel would have little incentive to consider withdrawing—a view widely shared in Lebanon. The converse proposition— that a cessation of resistance activities would induce Israel to withdraw—was often dismissed as laughably improbable, and not just by members of Hezbollah.

Neighboring Syria viewed the southern Lebanon situation as a fundamental strategic concern. To the extent that Israel held sway in the area, Syria's Lebanese flank was further exposed to an Israeli attack. Equally important, Syria insisted on firmly linking the fate of the South with that of the Israeli-occupied Golan Heights. When the Lebanese government tried to break that linkage in 1983, in the course of peace negotiations brokered by U.S. Secretary of State George Shultz, Damascus sabotaged the draft agreement. The May 17 agreement of 1983 would have ceded southern Lebanon to de-facto Israeli control in return for a formal Israeli military withdrawal. But the agreement contained a secret U.S.-Israeli provision in which the U.S. promised that the agreement would not be implemented without Syrian assent, which was not forthcoming. As Syria tightened its power grip in Lebanon, Lebanese officials repeatedly emphasized that the South was captive to Israeli-Syrian negotiations. A decade later, in 1993, when the Lebanese prime minister Rafiq Hariri tried to break the linkage, he was quickly yanked back in line. Hezbollah, meanwhile, backed Syria's contention that the prospect of a separate Lebanese deal with Israel was the route of weakness and would subordinate Lebanon to Israeli interests.

Hezbollah developed its own relations with various Palestinian groups, based in Lebanon, Palestine, and elsewhere. Fostering these ties was Israel's expulsion of four hundred alleged Palestinian militants to southern Lebanon in 1992. The Lebanese government forced the expelled Palestinians to stay in a contained area in the South that became, as many Palestinians later called it, "Hezbollah University," where Hezbollah indoctrinated its "students" in its perspective on resistance. Although many of the Palestinians were eventually allowed to return home, the ties built during that period have been largely sustained at Israel's cost.

Generally the Lebanese strongly resist the *tawtin*, or "naturalization," of its resident population of nearly four hundred thousand registered Palestinian refugees (although UN officials believe the actual number to be over 200,000, since many Palestinians have left for economic reasons). The Lebanese fear that integrating these refugees would destabilize Lebanon's delicate political balance, and they also bitterly recollect the Palestinian state-within-a-state that existed for more than a decade (until Israel's 1982 invasion). Most of the refugees have roots in Haifa and the villages of the Galilee, areas that are now very much part of the state of Israel. Although their camps were nominally disarmed in 1991, significant arms caches remain, and camps like ʿAin al-Hilwah, near Saida, are strongholds that the Lebanese army skirts. A number of armed Palestinian factions reportedly maintain cooperative relations with Hezbollah.

The civil war came to a close in Lebanon by the early 1990s, when all the militias, except Hezbollah, agreed to disband in accordance with the 1989 Ta'if accord. Hezbollah, which signed on to the accord only after the Iranian government gave its blessing, justified the maintenance of its armed forces by calling them "Islamic resistance" groups, not militias, committed to ending Israel's occupation. The forces were said to be needed to defend the country against the Israel-sponsored SLA. This position enjoyed wide, though not unanimous, support in Lebanon, where the Israeli occupation was seen as an impediment to the country's recovery.

The "Rules of the Game"

Practical "rules of the game" emerged, during the 1990s, between Hezbollah-led resistance forces versus the Israelis and their proxy, the SLA. Israel would not attack civilian targets in Lebanon, and the resistance would focus its actions on the Security Zone (Sobelman 2004). This modus vivendi was clearly articulated in an oral agreement in 1993, following Israel's "Operation Accountability," launched in July of that year. The 1993 agreement led to a temporary reduction in the intensity of violence and reprisal. But in 1996, after Hezbollah fired katyusha rockets into Israel in retaliation for the killing of Lebanese civilians, the Israel Defense Forces (IDF) again launched a major campaign into Lebanon. "Operation Grapes of Wrath," initiated in April of that year, was intended to undermine popular support for Hezbollah among the Lebanese, as well as to prompt Syria to rein in the organization. The strategy failed, largely as a result of the horrible slaughter at Qana, an ancient village some locals like to claim as the town cited in the Bible where Jesus turned water to wine (John 2:1–11). (In fact, the actual site is probably Cana in the Galilee.) At the UN base in Qana—a protected zone in international law—civilians sought refuge from IDF air and ground attacks. But rather than finding safety, 106 civilians were killed by Israeli artillery. Authoritative reports by the UN and Amnesty International challenged Israeli claims that the shelling of the UN base was unintentional, and these findings are well known in Lebanon.[2] However, the report of the UN Secretary-General's military adviser demonstrated that the Israeli shelling of the UNIFIL site was not accidental, and the thirteen shells that fell on the compound had exploded where they had been aimed.

[2] The UN report was prepared by Major General Franklin van Kappen, a Dutch officer serving on the staff of Secretary General Butrous Butrous Ghali. See Security Council document S/1996/137, May 7, 1996. See also Amnesty International, "Unlawful Killings during Operation 'Grapes of Wrath,'" July 1996, http:// www.amnesty.org/library/Index/engMDE150421996 (accessed October 21, 2006); and Human Rights Watch, "Israel/Lebanon: 'Operation Grapes of Wrath': The Civilian Victims" (September 1997).

No incident in recent memory has inspired more hatred for the Jewish state than the Qana attack. Close to the UN base, a memorial cemetery has been created where the victims are buried, and the site has become a popular memorial for many Lebanese to visit. Among middle-class professionals in *al-dahiyya* trips to Qana, usually with children in tow, are now common and have taken on the aspects of ritual. The site is festooned with banners (most in Arabic) accusing Israel of terrorism and genocide, and invoking sayings by some of the central figures in Shiʿism such as Imam Hussein. Many of the banners emphasize the loss of innocent blood and demand vengeance. One sign reads: "ʿQana is the Karbala [the site of Hussein's martyrdom in the year 680 c.e. [see chapter 3] of the twentieth century; it is a land made holy by the Lord Jesus and contaminated by the Zionist Satan (enemy of God)."

As CNN broadcast horrific pictures of mangled and burned civilians in the wake of this massacre, the then U.S. Secretary of State Warren Christopher succeeded in persuading all sides to abide once again by the same rules that had been in place since 1993. This time, however, the agreement was committed to an unsigned piece of paper. A noteworthy point is that in the course of negotiations Israel never challenged the right of Hezbollah to attack its soldiers in Lebanon, thus tacitly conceding that the IDF was an occupation force in the country. The April understanding brokered by Secretary Christopher specified that armed groups would not launch attacks against Israeli territory; Israel and its allies would not bombard civilians or civilian targets; both sides would commit themselves to avoid attacking civilians and launching attacks from civilian areas; and nothing in the agreement would prevent the right to self-defense. The agreement also provided for a monitoring group of the United States, France, Lebanon, Syria, and Israel to oversee the implementation of the agreement and to receive complaints of violations. The group would operate on the basis of unanimity and be based at Naquora, a southern coastal village and the site of an old customs house now used as the UNIFIL headquarters. From 1996 to 2000 the group operated as an effective mechanism for policing and reinforcing the rules of the game. UNIFIL has also functioned throughout its existence (from 1978 to the present) as a useful backchannel conduit for indirect communications between the belligerents.

One measure of the importance of the accepted rules was that both Israel and Hezbollah apologized for actions that fell outside the rules, as in November 1998, when Hezbollah apologized for a katyusha firing which it not only had not authorized but which it condemned. Israel has occasionally acted with marked restraint after suffering major casualties, on the argument that a given Hezbollah attack was permitted by the rules. It also bears emphasizing that Hezbollah resistance operations were mainly targeted against Israeli soldiers and the allied Lebanese militia, not against civilians. This is an important difference between Hezbollah in Lebanon and Hamas in Palestine. Whereas Hamas has intentionally targeted Israeli civilians, not least in suicide bombings, Hezbollah usually did not do so over the course of Israel's long occupation in Lebanon. Though shocking, perhaps, to many Western observers, the twelve suicide attacks launched by Hezbollah were all targeted against the occupation force and its allies, all legitimate resistance targets.

This is not to say that both sides always played by the "rules of the game." Both sides periodically disregarded time-honored principles of noncombatant immunity and proportionality. Resistance attacks on Israeli soldiers sometimes sparked indiscriminate Israeli reprisals that led to civilian deaths, especially after several Israeli soldiers had been killed. Hezbollah proved adept at moving within the rule box, which no doubt frustrated Israeli soldiers. The IDF, on a day-to-day basis, often adopted a policy of shoot first and ask questions later, which made daily life more than a bit risky for those living in the shadow of the Security Zone. Thus civilians were regularly killed "by accident" and in greater cumulative numbers than either members of the resistance, the IDF, or the SLA. In all, more than five hundred Lebanese and Palestinian civilians were killed in southern Lebanon from the time of the 1982 invasion to the Israeli withdrawal in 2000, or more than thirty times the number of Israeli civilian fatalities during this time. Human Rights Watch has carefully analyzed the deadly civilian toll (see, for example, Hilterman 1996).

The logic of Israel's "iron fist" was to punish Lebanese civilians disproportionately for the inability of the IDF to prevent attacks on its own soldiers and for retaliatory firing of katyusha rockets at Israel. Support for the resistance would wither, Israeli strategists thought, if they placed an awesome burden on the Lebanese, as, for example, when several hundred thousand people were roused from their homes and given a few hours to flee on threat of bombardment in April 1996. This proved to be a miscalculation, as many Lebanese believed that less resistance would induce Israel not to leave but to stay in the South.

Although Israel is anathema in the ideology of Hezbollah, there have been some mechanisms for negotiation, often through UNIFIL and sometimes through European states. The rules of the game allowed for both sides to conduct periodic, indirect negotiations for the return of prisoners and bodies.[3] Typically German negotiators have played an active role in the negotiations. Thus, in 1996, in return for the bodies of 2 IDF and 17 SLA soldiers, Israel released 45 detainees and the remains of 123 Lebanese. A similar exchange occurred in 1998, which was notable because one of the Lebanese bodies exchanged by Israel was that of Hadi Nasrallah, the son of Hezbollah Secretary-General Hasan Nasrallah. Hadi was killed in September 1997, in a raging battle with Israeli forces in southern Lebanon. (The elder Nasrallah's stoic acceptance of his son's death is often cited by party members as one of the reasons he is so highly esteemed.) The most sensational prisoner exchange was conducted as late as January 2004, when, in return for three bodies and one living retired lieutenant colonel who had been captured in Beirut, Israel released 23 Lebanese and 400 Palestinian prisoners. The Lebanese included Mustafa Dirani (captured in 1994) and Shaykh ʿAbdul Karim ʿUbayd (captured in 1989). These men had been held by Israel (in Camp 1391, one of the places Israeli officials do not talk about) as bargaining chips to gain information about Ron Arad, a long missing aviator who was captured alive in Lebanon, in 1986, but whose fate is now unknown.

The 2000 Israeli Withdrawal

In 1999 the retired chief of staff General Ehud Barak was elected prime minister of Israel. One of his campaign promises was that he would withdraw from Lebanon within twelve months of assuming office, either in conjunction with bilateral negotiations with Syria or unilaterally, with

---

[3] A typical statement of Hezbollah's position on Israel is provided by ʿAbdallah Qasir, a former member of parliament: "Direct negotiations are impossible because we do not recognize the existence of the State of Israel" (Al-Zaman, May 29, 2002).

the former the obvious preference. After several months of preparatory discussion between Israel and Syria in March 2000, President William Clinton flew to Geneva to meet with the Syrian president Hafez al-Asad, and, to the utter surprise of al-Asad and multitudes of Lebanese and Syrians, the negotiations failed. Barak refused (to Clinton's apparent annoyance) to release a pocket of Syrian land abutting Lake Tiberius, and the Syrians found this unacceptable. Al-Asad told Clinton, "I used to swim in that lake as a boy," and he insisted that all occupied Syrian land be returned. Israel then began focusing on unilateral withdrawal.

After the abortive Geneva meeting, the run-up to Israel's unilateral withdrawal began. Confusion abounded In Beirut and Damascus, with dire warnings of widespread chaos in Lebanon, including the slaughter of collaborators and bloody vendettas. Hasan Nasrallah's statements stood out for their clear analysis and calm assurances of Hezbollah's careful preparations for the aftermath of withdrawal. He emphasized that there would be no retaliatory killings or revenge attacks. In contrast, many other officials seemed like actors confused about their lines and unsure of their parts, so disconcerting and unwelcome was a voluntary Israeli exit.

Hezbollah maintained a position of calculated and coy ambiguity concerning the Israeli withdrawal. Although it was widely believed in Lebanon that the violence against the Jewish state would stop after the Israeli withdrawal, Hezbollah avoided saying so directly. Muhammad Ra'ad, the unflappable and very popular Hezbollah leader (and schoolteacher) from Nabatiya, who has been elected four times to the Lebanese parliament on the party's ticket, argued, in a 1996 interview with the author, that ambiguity increased Lebanese anxiety and the fear of Israel.

The withdrawal finally came on May 24, 2000. It was a time of extraordinary celebration in Lebanon, most especially in the South, and displaced residents immediately flooded into the South to repossess their liberated homes and villages. At the prison of al-Khiam, a horrendous detention center run by the SLA in close collaboration with Israel and the site of much mistreatment, even torture, people were literally tearing down prison doors with their bare hands to free the prisoners. In the rest of the countryside, apart from a few incidents that mainly involved beatings of collaborators—not even serious injuries, much less deaths— there was a remarkable degree of calm. Very little associated violence occurred, and certainly none of the revenge killings so widely anticipated. Many of the SLA people fled to Israel with their families. Those who remained were tried for collaboration and, typically, given sentences of four or five years, and in some cases advised not to return to their villages for a time. Overall, that time will be remembered as a remarkably orderly and humane period, especially when measured against the history of internecine violence that scarred Lebanon for much of the preceding few decades.

The summer following Israel's withdrawal, a serious debate arose within Hezbollah about whether to focus on Lebanese politics and themes, such as corruption, or to maintain the resistance posture both in Lebanon and the Middle East. After internal party discussions settled on the latter strategy, Nasrallah consulted with the Iranian *rakbar* (or leader) Ayatollah ʿAli Khamenei, who gave his blessing to continue the resistance, especially in the Israeli-Palestinian theater. Hezbollah found a clever pretext to continue paramilitary operations against Israel by attacking Israeli patrols on farmland adjoining the village of Shebaa, a disputed territory in the Israeli-occupied Golan Heights (called "Har Dov"

Mount David by Israelis) that Lebanon claims as its own. Israeli military presence there allowed Hezbollah to maintain a military posture on the pretext that the Israeli withdrawal from Lebanon had not been complete.

During the period between the Israeli withdrawal of May 2000 and the explosion of war in July 2006 (examined in chapter 6) one Israeli civilian was killed by Hezbollah weapons, and five more were killed in a Palestinian operation that may have had Hezbollah's help. Nine Israeli soldiers died in Hezbollah attacks in the contested farms area, and eight others were killed in six clashes along the "Blue Line" demarcated by the UN after Israel's withdrawal. Some of the attacks were in retaliation for Israeli-caused deaths in Lebanon. At least twenty-one Israeli soldiers were also wounded. The total of seventeen Israeli soldiers killed during a six-year period contrasted to an average of twenty-five Israeli soldiers who died annually during Israel's occupation of southern Lebanon, according to Israeli Justice Minister Haim Ramon.

Harassing fire, aggressive patrolling, and heated rhetoric by both sides marked the entire period. On the Lebanese side of the border billboards facing Israel exhibited slogans in Hebrew, stating, for example, "If you come back, we'll come back." Hezbollah delighted in sponsoring cross-border taunting and stone throwing at Israeli military positions. In fact, piles of rocks were conveniently available adjacent to the Fatima gate, through which Israel had often entered Lebanon.

Generally, however, this six-year period was a relatively quiet, peaceful time by historical standards, and this was frequently commented on by Israeli officials prior to the summer of 2006. The more serious clashes tended to occur in the Shebaa area of the occupied Golan Heights. This period is important to consider because it indicated that maintaining stability across this hostile border is neither impossible nor infeasible. Indeed, the rules of the game were well understood by both Israel and its Hezbollah foe.

In October 2000 Hezbollah launched an operation in the Shebaa Farms area that led to the ambush and capture of three Israeli soldiers. The captives all died, either on the spot or later from their wounds, their bodies only returned in the January 2004 exchange. After that operation Israel resumed the routine violations of Lebanese airspace and territorial waters that it had ceased in May or June 2000, when it was seeking UN certification of its withdrawal under the terms of Security Council Resolution 425. From October 2000 on, Israeli war planes regularly flew over Lebanese territory, with sonic booms over Beirut, intelligence collecting drones, and similar incursions. In time, Hezbollah began firing anti-aircraft weapons at Israeli planes violating Lebanese airspace, but as they were firing southward, in the direction the planes were coming from, the spent ammunition rounds would land in Israel. Hezbollah also began firing Katyusha rockets, mostly into the occupied Golan Heights, with a few episodes of Katyusha firings into Israel proper as well. Although several dozen incidents occurred over the last six years, in almost every case, according to Israeli sources, the culprits were Palestinian fedayeen, not Hezbollah.

The periodic episodes of violence during this period occurred in the Shebaa Farms area, Israeli-occupied territory. The rules were so well established, in fact, that officials on both sides were periodically quoted as saying that such and such a military action was within the "rules of the game."

Israel's withdrawal from southern Lebanon was followed closely by the eruption of the second Intifada, or Palestinian uprising, in September 2000. That Intifada movement clearly was partially inspired by Hezbollah's stunning success. In 2000 and 2001 Hezbollah flags flew in many Palestinian camps in the West Bank and Gaza, and Hezbollah played a role in training anti-Israeli Palestinians and a minor role in supplying them. The major exception were the arms that Iran shipped on the *Karine-A*, which included a Hezbollah crewman and was intercepted by Israel in January 2002 (the incident apparently encouraged George Bush to pin the "axis-of-evil" label on Iran). Otherwise, Nasrallah carefully stressed that the job of liberating Palestine belonged to the Palestinians, just as the job of liberating the Golan Heights belonged to Syria. Even so, the level of incitement from Hezbollah was very high. The Hezbollah television station, al-Manar ("the Beacon"), beamed terrestrial and satellite propaganda to many avid Palestinian viewers. The number of viewers had peaked in 2001, and dropped in 2003 to 8 percent, compared to an audience of more than 50 percent for the CNN-clone al-Jazeerah. Al-Manar was the sixth most popular satellite station in the Arab world, trailing far behind al-Arabiya as well as al-Jazeerah, according to a January 2006 poll by the U.S. firm Zogby International.

In Lebanon, meanwhile, the Hezbollah leadership was unanimously persuaded, as were most of the supporters, that its demonstrated military prowess and accumulating military arsenal provided by Iran and Syria was successfully deterring Israel from invading Lebanon again, or from bombarding Lebanon as it had done so often in the past. In July 2006, however, Hezbollah was to discover that its deterrent shield was not as intimidating as it imagined.

Chapter 5
Playing Politics

The Bahman hospital in the southern suburbs of Beirut, one of a multitude of social services connected with Shi'i foundations, religious figures or political groups such as Hezbollah. Copyright A. R. Norton, 2006.

Lebanon has a curious electoral system that is intended to accommodate its mélange of confessional spirits, diverse regional interests, and personal rivalries. Voters have gone to the polls every four years (except for the civil war years of 1975 to 1990) to vote for members of parliament. As a result of the Ta'if accord of 1989, which marked the end of the civil war, seats are divided equally between Muslim and Christians, in contrast to the prior distribution that favored Christians by a 6 to 5 ratio. The 128 parliamentary seats are subdivided along confessional lines: 27 seats each for the three largest sects—Shi'a, Sunni, and Maronites—with most districts confessionally mixed. Voters cast ballots for each available seat in the district regardless of the seat's confessional label. The system promotes local inter-sectarian alliances to persuade voters to cast votes for an entire alliance list rather than picking and choosing individual candidates. Voters are not without discretionary choices, such as the fairly common al-tashtib, or "crossing out"; the voter scratches out the undesired candidate and then votes for the remaining members of a list rather than for the whole list. On rare occasions voters even pick and choose among lists, writing in the names of their preferred candidates.

When the civil war in Lebanon finally ended, elections for parliament had not been held in eighteen years. Only about two-thirds of the parliamentarians from the 1975 Chamber of Deputies survived to see the chaos and bloodshed end. As an ostensible transitional step, parliamentary appointments in 1991 filled forty seats. This unpopular technique was, in part, a device championed by Syria to seed the new parliament with pro-Damascus militia leaders who had gained power during the civil war. The appointments coincided with the consolidation of Syria's grip on Lebanon, which was formalized in May 1991 with a Treaty of Brother-

hood, Cooperation, and Coordination. The treaty legiti-
mated a heavy Syrian hand, particularly in defense and security realms.

The first post–civil war elections were finally held in
1992. Unsuccessful efforts to formally explore the monitoring of balloting were launched by the International Peace
Academy, the Norwegian Institute of International Affairs,
and the Centre for Lebanese Studies, which included such
highly respected figures as the late Katchiq Babikian, who
had served with distinction as Lebanon's minister of justice.
These efforts—which count this author as one of the initia-
tors—proved fruitless when it became clear that neither
Beirut nor Damascus had the slightest inclination to welcome foreign oversight. Syria's covert manipulation of
these elections included interference in the composition of
candidate lists and drawing up electoral districts with a view
to isolating opposition voices and insuring the victory of
Syria's allies.

Many Lebanese Christians, especially Maronites, were
deeply resentful of Syria's overbearing role, and they moved
to boycott the elections. As a result of the boycott, voter
participation rates of less than 10 percent were not uncommon in predominantly Christian districts and, thanks to the
absence of many Christian voters at the polls, pro-Syrian
candidates were swept into office in many districts where
they might otherwise have faced tougher competition.

Hezbollah's Decision to Participate

The 1992 elections posed a crucial question for Hezbollah:
Should the party adhere to its previous denunciation of the
confessional electoral system as corrupt, and reject partici-

pation, or seize the moment and compete in the election? The very idea that Hezbollah would participate in Lebanese elections had been rejected outright by its leaders in the 1980s. However, the most influential Shiʿi cleric in Lebanon, Sheikh Muhammad Husain Fadlallah, had been espousing a pro-election position for years. Fadlallah argued that, because revolutionary transition to Islamic rule and an Islamic state was impossible in the diverse Lebanese society, gradual reformation was necessary. And that, insisted Fadlallah, required participating in the political system. As Jamal Sankari reveals in his intricately detailed biography of the pragmatic Fadlallah, the Shiʿi cleric emphasized the need to come to a modus vivendi with the state rather than remain outside the political system and judge it as abhorrent in strictly Islamic terms. Other leading Lebanese clerics less closely associated with Hezbollah made similar points. The late Sheikh Muhammad Mahdi Shams al-Din, a cleric revered for his intellectual depth and leader and president of the Supreme Islamic Shiʿi Council from 1978 to 2001, told me emphatically, in a 1997 interview, that it is necessary for Islamist parties to take into account the power of contending secular forces. Shams al-Din emphasized that political compromises are often necessary.

Hezbollah's deputy secretary-general Naʿim Qassem, who began his involvement in Lebanese politics, like many party members, as a member of Amal in the 1970s, has offered an insider account's of the "deep internal debate" that preceded the 1992 elections. Twelve leading members were deputized to debate the issue, including Qassem; Nasrallah, who had replaced the assassinated ʿAbbas al-Musawi just the year before; and Subhi Tufayli, the president of the ephemeral Islamic Republic of Baalbek (the major town in the northern

Beqaa valley) in 1984, who rose to become Hezbollah's first secretary-general in 1989. The debate turned on three key questions. From the standpoint of Islamic law, was participation in a "non-Islamic" government legitimate? Should ideology bend to practical interests? And would Hezbollah, by its participation, be co-opted into a secular political system, thereby deserting its principles and Islamic vision? Tufayli, known not for eloquence but for rash stridency, insisted (and continues to insist) that by running for office the party would be "selling out," and that Hezbollah would be transformed (*tahawwal*) from a revolutionary force to a tame political participant. Other members sought a compromise, suggesting that party members should run as individuals, not in the name of the party.

The legitimacy issue was referred to Iran's Ali Khamenei, who succeeded Ruhollah Khomeini as the supreme legal authority (wali al-faqih), in 1989, upon Khomeini's death. In Shiʿism individuals choose a respected and learned scholar as their *marjiʿ al-taqlid*, or "source of emulation," their ultimate authority on Islamic law. In Iran, Ayatollah Khomeini had taken this principle a major step beyond accepted practice by arguing for the necessity of a supreme jurisconsult, a distinguished Shiʿi scholar who would not just resolve religious and legal matters but also would be the nation's ultimate political authority. Thus Iran's ʿAli Khamenei, considered by Hezbollah to be its "official" marjaʿi, gave his blessing to the possibility of Hezbollah's participation in Lebanese elections, thereby strongly supporting the pro-election wing and also providing grist for Hezbollah's critics in Lebanon who question its national identity. Incidentally, most rank-and-file Hezbollah members and supporters emulate Iraq's Ayatollah ʿAli al-Sistani or Lebanon's Ayatollah

Fadlallah, who are both important thinkers in the Shiʿi world. The Iranian leader is simply not taken very seriously as a religious scholar, but he enjoys obvious and important political authority.

In the end, ten men embraced running for office, whereas two, including Tufayli, rejected the idea and left in a fury over the decision, which, at the delegation's conclusion, was again submitted to Khamenei for approval.

The determination to enter Lebanese politics for the first time was widely popular in the Shiʿi community. Adherents of both Amal and Hezbollah had always suffered a deep-seated sense of political disenfranchisement, so the prospect of gaining representation offered hope of growing political empowerment. Of course, some viewed the elections merely as means for greater access to political benefits, literally allocations (*muhassasat*), which refers to access to government jobs, contracts, licenses, or permits, among other goods that are typically allocated along confessional lines in Lebanon. But officials debating the question also saw strategic benefits to winning elected office. Hezbollah would gain both official recognition as a political institution in Lebanon as well as a public podium, and would also be able to influence the budget to its constituents' advantage. By being inside the political system, Hezbollah might also be able to shape political dialogue to its benefit, as well as head off problematic initiatives. In the end, therefore, ideology bent to pragmatism, and Nasrallah announced, on July 3, 1992, that the party would compete in that summer's elections.

In the 1992 elections Hezbollah and its non-Shiʿi electoral allies (often from Baalbek, where Shiʿa comprise only about half the population) captured twelve seats in the Lebanese parliament, including eight Shiʿi seats. With only small variations from one election to the next, Hezbollah has maintained its electoral standing, routinely winning around 10 percent of all parliamentary seats. And although the Hezbollah leadership sometimes made questionable use of Islamic doctrine in each election—for example, the leadership's repeated declaration that Hezbollah members were legally required, as though commanded by Allah (*taklif al-shar'i*), to support the party—most striking about Hezbollah's political campaigns is the extent to which nonreligious themes are habitually emphasized. The party electoral platform emphasizes battling economic exploitation and underdevelopment, inequities in the political system, personal freedom and opportunity, and, of course, security. Hezbollah's electoral strategy does not dwell explicitly on religious themes at all, in stark contrast to, for example, Christian fundamentalist groups in the United States.

For many years the central preoccupation of the Shi'i community has been the Israeli military occupation of southern Lebanon. Hezbollah has regularly capitalized on its role in the resistance in its campaign slogans, as in 1996 when some of its posters read: "They resist with their blood, resist with your vote." Particularly in 2000, the year of Israel's unilateral withdrawal, Hezbollah might have won four or five more seats at the expense of Amal but the *saqf al-suri*, or the "Syrian ceiling," was widely understood to set an upper limit on the number of Hezbollahi candidates permitted to compete. The ceiling reflected Syria's usual balancing act in Lebanese politics, with the result that, in 2000, an Amal-Hezbollah alliance—the Resistance and Development Bloc—won all twenty-three available seats in southern Lebanon and more than a quarter of all seats in parliament (table 5.1).

TABLE 5.1
Parliamentary Election Results for 27 Shi'i Seats

| | Hezbollah | Sunni | Non-Shi'i Hezbollah allies | | | |
			Greek Catholic	Maronite	Amal	Others*
1992	8	2	1	1	9	10
1996	7	1		1	8	12
2000	9	2		1	6	12
2005	11	2		1	11	5

* Secular parties and traditional elites.

Municipal Elections

Unlike the parliamentary elections, in which Syria has meddled incessantly, municipal elections have largely been left alone. Most election observers have noted the relative fairness of Lebanon's municipal elections, especially compared to its recent parliamentary elections, which have been transparently manipulated by the government and by Syria. The stakes are lower, the contests are harder to stage-manage, and it is not as easy to fool local voters if their choices are thwarted. Thus recent elections in municipalities provide a useful gauge of the popularity of Hezbollah and its rivals. These elections also illustrate the pragmatic political bargains that Hezbollah has often made with ideological opposites, such as the avowedly secular Syrian Social Nationalist Party and even the Communist Party. This is a striking contrast to the 1980s when Hezbollah fought pitched battles with the former party and reputedly killed dozens of members of the latter.

The municipal elections in the summer of 1998 were the first local elections in more than three decades. Hezbollah

Chapter 5

demonstrated its strong base in Beirut, especially in *al-dahi-yya* (the suburbs) where it soundly thrashed the candidates of Nabih Berri's Amal Party. In the massive Beirut suburbs of Burj al-Barajnah and al-Ghubayri, Hezbollah slates carried the day. Ghubayri has become an interesting example of Hezbollah's capacity to govern at the local level. It is the largest town in the suburbs and it has been singled out by the United Nations for its exemplary efforts at providing low-income housing.[1]

In Ghubayri the 1998 Hezbollah municipal election slate was led by Muhammad Sa'id al-Khansa, a scion of a large and much respected clan that dominates the busy trade in automobile parts. The al-Khansas are represented across a rich variety of businesses far removed from tires and transmissions, including the haute couture studio of Jamil al-Khansa, which is well known in Paris and the Gulf. Like many other extended Lebanese families, the al-Khansas boast a government-chartered family association, which give needy members of the large extended family subsidies and loans for foreign education, sophisticated medical attention, or disaster relief. With hundreds of clan members, the al-Khansa family enjoys considerable electoral clout at the municipal level. Their Husseiniya—which, as discussed

---

[1] The suburb is also notable for another reason, well known to Lebanese, namely, it is the site of Monoprix, which not only offers a nice selection of foods and clothing but arguably the best liquor store in the country. The store is an important source of tax income for Ghubayri, because the municipality maneuvered deftly to prevent the national government from having all the tax revenues flow directly to the state. In 2000, when this writer asked the head of the municipality, a widely admired member of Hezbollah, about the sale of alcohol, normally prohibited in Islam, his response implied pragmatic tolerance. At first he noted that many Lebanese Christians shop in Monoprix, and Christians face no prohibition on alcohol. Then, when pushed a bit, he chuckled and said that many of the Shi'a who had worked in West Africa "drank like fish." With a laugh he said, "That's their choice."

in chapter 3, is the building used annually during Muharram for the commemoration of Imam Hussein's martyrdom at Karbala—is one of the largest in *al-dahiyya*, which makes it an important political and social site, as well as an important gathering place for community events and rites of passage, such as funerals.

Although parliamentary speaker and Amal leader Nabih Berri's slate performed poorly in *al-dahiyya*, Amal performed credibly in the South and in the Beqaa valley, winning control of Tyre, a movement stronghold. Hezbollah held its own by capturing the southern municipality of al-Nabatiya In the southern town of Sarafand, Hezbollah aligned with the secular Syrian Social Nationalist Party to win shared control of the municipal council. In the underdeveloped northern Beqaa valley, Amal captured Baalbek through a deal with secular parties and farmers, and Hezbollah captured Hirmil to the north. Although Baalbek is often thought of as the bedrock of Hezbollah, the city's population is only half Shiʿi Muslim, with Sunnis and Christians accounting for the rest. The Beqaa valley also features one of Hezbollah's most formidable regional political rivals, former Hezbollah secretary-general Subhi Tufayli, who has accused his former party of doting on the South to the neglect of the suffering Beqaa. Tufayli has built a large constituency in the Beqaa valley, where the economy remains heavily dependent upon agriculture, including illicit drug cultivation.

The Revolt of the Hungry

By the mid-1990s Lebanon's agricultural sector was suffering from the flood of cheap produce from Syria. (Syria's exploitation of its free access to the Lebanese economy ended only in 2005.) The hardship this caused to the valley's farmers spawned a mood of angry discontent that Tufayli helped to inflame. Tufayli famously opposed Hezbollah's decision to run in Lebanese elections, but by 1997 he announced that he would be running for election in the 1998 municipal races. Then, on July 4, 1997, he organized rallies that, while banned by the government, were still attended by several thousand followers. Tufayli's populist platform—the *thawrat al-jiyaa*, or "revolution of the hungry"—included demands for job creation; crop subsidies; free education, electricity, and water; and state benefits and pensions for service with the resistance in lieu of army service. The platform implicitly criticized Hezbollah for failing its needy constituents and prompted well-founded concern on the part of the Hezbollah leadership, which understood the potential attraction of a "revolution of the hungry" in the dense Shi'i suburbs of Beirut.

Tufayli's seeds of revolution bore electoral fruit. In the 1998 municipal elections Tufayli captured his hometown as well as neighboring Tarayya but split a large adjoining village with Hezbollah.

Tufayli was indicted for killing an army lieutenant, in January 1998, yet he is still on the scene, accusing Hezbollah of being a tool of Syrian foreign policy and a servant of Israel, and charging that Hasan Nasrallah is an intelligence agent for Iran. He explains, not unjustifiably, that his freedom of action is the result of his huge following, which acts as a check on Hezbollah's influence. As the Tufayli episode illustrates, Hezbollah cannot afford to take its electoral success in Lebanon for granted.

In the next set of municipal elections, in 2004, Hezbollah offered a more palatable political program in the Beqaa and Hirmil regions than it had in 1998. Building on a proven track record of efficient governance, and profiting from its leading role in the liberation of the South, the party was a steamroller in both the Beqaa and in the Beirut suburbs, as well as in the South. The voters' enthusiasm for Hezbollah also had been bolstered by the German-mediated release, in January 2004, of four hundred Palestinian and twenty-three Lebanese prisoners from Israeli jails in return for a captured retired lieutenant colonel and the bodies of three Israeli soldiers. Not only did Hezbollah capture the municipality of Baalbek, but it gained control of twenty-six other local governments in the Beqaa where it lost only three contests. Throughout Lebanon it topped its main rival, Amal, by 2 to 1 in local government seats won.

The Rich Texture of Shi'i Institutions

The Lebanese government offers paltry social welfare services for its citizens, and the few that are available are heavily concentrated within Beirut. A broad range of services are sorely needed in *al-dahiyya*, where per capita income is one-fifth to one-sixth of the national average ($6,000 prior to the 2006 war). With no safety net of state-provided social services, life has traditionally been very hard indeed for those without prosperous extended families. But the glaring lack of non-family—based support services began to ease in recent decades, at least in the Shi'i community, owing in part to the vision of the Shi'i cleric Muhammad Hussein Fadlallah. During the civil war Fadlallah spoke about the necessity of creating a *dawlat al-insan*, or "human state," that would provide the resources for people to help themselves and one another. Fadlallah's concept has inspired the emergence of many private social service associations mostly serving the Shi'i community. Some are linked directly to Fadlallah or to other leading sayyids, institutions, and parties, notably including the Musa al-Sadr Foundation, the Supreme Islamic Shiʿi Council, the Amal movement, and Hezbollah. Husseiniyas, some built by families, others funded by municipalities or benevolent trusts (*awqaf*; sing., *waqf*) are often important centers for associational life, and in smaller villages they are often the only site for social assistance. Anthropologist Lara Deeb (2006, 170) recently quoted a Shiʿi woman in the Beirut suburbs who observed, "Before, there was nothing here, not a single *jamʿiya* (charitable organization), nothing." Although not literally true, the statement does underline the paucity of *jamʿiyaat*, or associations, only a few decades ago.

The present abundance of associations in the Shiʿi community is an essential part of the construction of a modern, confident notion of identity, and a spirit of activism and volunteerism (discussed in chapter 3) stands in contrast to earlier, rampant acceptance of deprivation among the Shiʿa.

Fadlallah has been particularly effective as an institution builder. In 1976 he was named *wakil*, or deputy, by the Najaf-based Ayatollah al-Azma Sayyid Abu al-Qasim al-Khuʿi, who until his death in 1992 was one of the most revered of the marjaʿi. ("sources" of law). As al-Khuʿi's *wakil*, Fadlallah was entrusted to collect donations on his behalf and use those donations for good purpose in Lebanon. Thus Fadlallah oversaw cooperatively with Musa al-Sadr and Muhammad Mahdi Shams al-Din the Imam Khuʿi Orphanage (begun ca. 1963 in Beirut), as well as the Bahman Hospital in *al-dahiyya*. With the death of his colleagues, these important institutions were absorbed by Fadlallah's massive Benevolent Charity Society (Jamiʿiyyat al-Mabarrat al-Khayriya, created in 1978). Fadllallah's Social Services Office (Maktab al-Khadimat al-Ijtimaaʿiya) is also highly respected. These institutions employ several thousand people and include many volunteers.

Although wealthy Shiʿa, including émigrés and rich Shiʿa in the Gulf, are often important donors, most of the jamʿiyy-aat depend heavily on local fund-raising and donations or generate income themselves. As Lara Deeb (2006, 89) notes, Fadlallah's rich complex of institutions includes businesses such as gas stations, a publishing house, a photo-copy store, a factory for religiously permissible or halal foods (such as meat that has been slaughtered according to Islamic rules—similar to Kosher standards), and a computer store. Individual donations include alms (zakat) that may be paid in kind, such as gifts of food for the poor; Ramadan gifts, khums (a fifth of one yearly income after meeting living expenses), half of which is paid to one's marjaʿ or wakil and the other half to a descendant of the prophet or sayyid, and ad hoc donations by the faithful (sadaqat). Respected jamʿiyaat are often authorized by several marjaʿis to collect donations on their behalf. It is not unusual for as much as two million dollars to be collected on a single night during Ramadan.

Also noteworthy is the Imam Sadr Foundation based in the southernmost city of Tyre and run by Rabab al-Sadr, the sister of Imam Musa. In addition to the Burj al-Barajnah vocational school for boys, Sitt Rabab heads an extremely impressive vocational institute for women, which is often much admired by visitors.

Hezbollah offers an array of social services to its constit-uents that include construction companies, schools, hospi-tals, dispensaries, and micro-finance initiatives (notably al-Qard al-Hasan, literally the "good loan," that began making loans in 1984 and now offers about 750 small loans a month). These tend to be located in predominantly Shi'i areas, but some serve anyone requesting help. Hezbollah hospital and clinic staff also treat all walk-in patients, regardless of political views or their sect, for only a small fee.

Much of the funding for the social and medical infrastructure is raised domestically, but Hezbollah also receives significant subsidies from Iran. The amounts are often estimated at $100 million a year, but, in fact, they vary widely, depending on the political climate in Iran. A significant portion of Iranian support is for Hezbollah's militia wing. Several of the Hezbollah-sponsored societies are actually branches of Iranian organizations or were initially created by Iran. Hence the large Islamic Charity Emdad (ICEC) was created in 1987 with Iranian financial support but today depends heavily on volunteer labor. Deeb (2006, 90) notes that of 440 Emdad employees only about 90 were paid, and many paid employees donate a significant amount of unpaid labor. The Martyr's Association was created in 1982 by Khomeini and operates as a sister organization to an Iranian organization of the same name, as does the Association for the Wounded. Other organizations were created by Hezbollah, more notably the Jihad al-Binaa⁽ Development Organization, which has literally reconstructed and repaired much of the damage wrought by war. The Hezbollah Women's Committee and the Islamic Health Committee are also important groups.

The Amal movement also provides various services to its supporters, including schools, clinics, and hospitals, some of which rival individual Hezbollah facilities. Amal is able to draw on the donations of its membership and some well-to-do benefactors, but it lacks a generous benefactor such as the role Iran plays for Hezbollah. The Amal movement's institutions generally have had much less impact on Lebanese society than either Hezbollah's institutions or those connected with leaders such as Ayatollah Fadlallah. Of course, as speaker of the parliament, Amal's leader, Nabih Berri, is an important source of government patronage, which is often harnessed to Amal's purposes.

A Shiʿi friend, in 2004, told me that, "there are no needy people in *al-dahiyya*," implying that the rich fabric of social and charitable organizations meet the needs of people who would otherwise be impoverished. A safety net exists today that simply was not there before, and many Shiʿa take pride in knowing that they have helped to build it. Nonetheless segments of the community remain in distress, as the example of Subhi Tufayli's Beqaa-based "Revolt of the Hungry" demonstrated.

The social services institutions that do exist in the Shiʿi community were put to an extraordinary test in 2006 by the Israeli attacks that targeted broad swaths of the Shiʿi community and left as many as fifteen thousand homes destroyed or badly damaged. The severe, extensive damage obviously has overwhelmed even Hezbollah's services framework, but the party's prompt action to meet its constituents' needs, in August 2006 (discussed in chapter 6), is a vivid example of the competence and professionalism that has won Hezbollah extensive support among many Lebanese Shiʿa.

More important than the specifics of any one association is the evidence that a palpable sense of community and religious commitment (*iltizam*) now exist which emphasize that a mark of faith is to offer a helping hand to others and participate in the community. Ayatollah Fadlallah is known for

111

capturing this ethos in his comment that he does not want followers but rather partners. It is impossible to appreciate the striking durability and loyalty that modern Shiʿi groups, such as Hezbollah (or comparable groups in Iraq, for instance), generate unless one understands that their strength derives from the strong social fabric that they have woven over the years.

Chapter 6
From Celebration to War

The Beirut suburbs of Haret Hreik on the morning of August 14, 2006, a few hours after a cease-fire in the 2006 war. Copyright Ali Safa, 2006.

The exuberant nationwide Lebanese celebration of Israel's 2000 withdrawal began to run out of steam within a couple of years, particularly outside the formerly occupied region. People still made the trek to the large village of al-Khiam, a couple of miles north of the Israeli town of Metulla, where they visited the infamous Israeli prison from the period of the occupation. The prison, formerly a French military barracks built during the League of Nations mandate in pre-independence Syria and Lebanon (1920–43), had been a thoroughly miserable place to be jailed. Until Israel bombed it during the summer of 2006, it was preserved more or less as it was on May 24, 2000, the day of the Israeli withdrawal from Lebanon, when the guards—members of the Israeli-funded proxy militia—fled and neighboring villagers forced the cells open. Visitors would come to gawk at the poorly lit, cramped cells, the frayed toothbrushes, improvised eating utensils, a "dispensary" that seemed more a janitor's closet than a medical facility, and a metal utility pole to which inmates were occasionally tied and beaten with electric cables (on two occasions to death). After leaving al-Khiam, visitors might make their way to the much-bombed, ruined, but still awesome crusader fortress, Chateau de Beaufort, with its sweeping vistas of the Galilee, or to a memorial cemetery for the victims of the shelling of Qana in 1996. En route, Hezbollah flags were common, interspersed with billboards honoring martyrs and schematics recounting resistance operations. Voyeuristic sightseeing aside, many Lebanese wanted to "live and let live," as one founding member of Hezbollah said to this author in May 2000. Israel was gone, and most Lebanese had no desire to fight other people's battles. For five consecutive years, on May 25, the government sponsored an annual commemoration of the liberation of the South, but that stopped in 2006, as if Lebanon's political elites had decided it was time to move on.

In the summer of 2000, before the second Palestinian intifadah erupted in September, and before Hezbollah began its campaign against the few remaining Israeli forces in the Shebaa Farms area of the occupied Golan Heights. Hasan Nasrallah was a regional, even international celebrity. He was rewarded by a visit from UN Secretary-General Kofi Annan. His ordering of the operation that led to the capture, in October, of three Israeli soldiers in the Shebaa area possessed a clear logic; like Israel, which had earlier captured Shiʿi fighters in the South as bargaining chips, Hezbollah now had bargaining chips of its own. The chips were exploited to full effect when, with German help, a deal was reached, in January 2004, to give up the bodies of the three captured soldiers (who were either dead when captured, or succumbed to their wounds) and to return an Israeli reserve lieutenant colonel reputedly lured to Beirut under murky, apparently illicit circumstances. In an Israeli procedure clothed in secrecy, the officer was charged with unspecified crimes and agreed to a plea bargain by which he was sentenced to the time that he was held in captivity by Hezbollah.[1] In exchange for the Israeli captives who were released, Israel freed 423 prisoners, of whom 23 were Lebanese and the remainder Palestinians. The prisoner exchange was a moment of triumph, which, as we saw in the previous chapter, paid off a few months later in sweeping victories for Hezbollah in the 2004 municipal elections.

The occasional skirmish in Shebaa often obscured the fact that, as noted in chapter 4, for the six years following

---

[1] For some details surrounding this intriguing episode, see the *Jerusalem Post*, October 23, 2003; and http://www.israelnationalnews.com/news.php3?id=66727.

Israel's exit from Lebanon in the spring of 2000, the border was more or less quiet. This confounded the predictions of many experts who had predicted that the Israeli exit would leave a vacuum that would likely be filled by mayhem. During these six years of relative stability, nine Israeli soldiers were killed in the Shebaa Farms area. Another eight Israeli soldiers were killed along the "Blue Line" demarcated by the UN after Israel's withdrawal (some on Lebanese soil and others on Israeli soil). A total of seventeen Israeli soldiers were lost during the six-year period compared to about twenty-five per year during the occupation. As far as Israeli civilian casualties were concerned, during this entire six-year period, there was only one Israeli civilian fatality, a teenaged boy who was killed by an anti-aircraft round fired by Hezbollah. (There was also an operation in 2002 involving two Palestinian fighters who managed to cross the border and ambush and kill six Israelis—five civilians and a soldier. Even though Hezbollah was not directly involved, it is difficult to imagine anyone crossing the border without some level of Hezbollah cooperation. If these are counted, the total Israeli civilian deaths were six, or one per year.) Lebanese and Palestinian civilian deaths during this same period included a shepherd killed by Israeli gunfire, and a preponderance of deaths caused by landmines and cluster bombs left as a legacy of Israel's operations and attacks.

As the euphoria of the Israeli withdrawal began to fade, so did the adulation for Hezbollah. Critics arose who argued that the organization's periodic attacks on Israel, even if confined to the Shebaa Farms area, were reckless and unjustified. In one of his many outspoken newspaper articles, Gibran Tueni, the publisher of Lebanon's leading newspaper and a widely read critic of both Syria and Hezbollah, asked: "Who authorized Nasrallah to represent all the Lebanese, to make decisions for them and to embroil them in something they don't want to be embroiled in? Did Nasrallah appoint himself secretary general of all the Lebanese and the whole Arab world?" (*an-Nahar*, May 5, 2003). Tueni was only one of many who accused Nasrallah of being intoxicated with his own fame.

Another sign of discord involving Hezbollah at this time (2003) occurred when Nayif Krayem, the well-known director of the party's television station al-Manar, was dismissed from his post because he seemed to be loyal to Ayatollah Muhammad Hussein Fadlallah, whose moral influence Hezbollah had come to distrust. All this arose indirectly from Hezbollah's criticism of flagellation and similar religious practices in the al-ʿAshura commemorations, as discussed in chapter 4. Indeed, Hezbollah's position is complementary to that of many senior *mujtahids* who argue that these rituals detract from Islam and divert people from appropriately contemplating the Muharram tragedy. Before his dismissal, Krayem wrote an article making the same points, using quotations from the revered Iranian Ayatollah Mortazza Mutaharri as support. The reason for his dismissal was not his citation of Mutaharri but the suspicion that he was using the citations as a smoke screen to obscure his debt to the ideas of Fadlallah, who, as previously seen in chapter 5, is the most influential Shiʿi thinker and cleric in Lebanon. Krayem categorically denied the charges in an extraordinary series of newspaper articles in the Arabic press. Although frequently and incorrectly described in the West as Hezbollah's "spiritual guide," Fadlallah's relationship with Hezbollah, although civil, is often strained and tense. Krayem's 2003 firing should be understood to reflect not only the party leadership's distrust of Fadlallah's moral influence but their overall siege mentality following a couple of years of basking in adulation after the Israeli withdrawal.

As the U.S.-British invasion of Iraq loomed in early 2003, Hezbollah wanted to step out of the crosshairs. The party cooled its rhetoric, its episodic taunts along the border with Israel, and its strikes at Israeli army positions in the Shebaa region. Although many Lebanese Shi'a adored him, Nasrallah won few plaudits from Iraqi co-religionists when he argued against toppling Saddam Hussein and his regime, and instead urged the Iraqis to convene a national reconciliation conference, with elections and the formation of a new government. There was no rush among Iraqi Shi'a and Kurds to embrace Nasrallah's unsolicited proposal; the plan only evoked their criticism, as they viewed the suggestion as laughable that the Iraqi Baathist regime would conciliate itself out of existence. In the United States, meanwhile, the spring of its Iraq invasion in 2003 was a period of unfettered optimism not yet undermined by the Bush administration's miscalculations or the nightmare of violence that haunts Iraq still. Nasrallah's trenchant assessment proved prescient: "We tell the United States, don't expect that the people of this region will welcome you with roses and jasmine. The people of this region will welcome you with rifles, blood, and martyrdom operations. We are not afraid of the American invaders, and we will keep saying 'death to America'" (al-Intiqad, March 14, 2003). Such prophetic statements did nothing to diminish U.S. hostility toward Hezbollah.

Nasrallah had his own, self-interested reasons to oppose the Americans. This became clear during the first weeks after the Iraq invasion, when the euphoria of a quick succession of victories led to speculation, in and around the Bush administration, about further, immanent military action to snatch the "low-hanging fruit" elsewhere in the region to exploit America's apparent strategic momentum. The threatening chatter, which received lively play in the Beirut media, referred most commonly to toppling the government in Syria, attacking Hezbollah in Lebanon, and the rather fanciful notion that the U.S. might sponsor an opposition uprising in Iran to topple the Islamic regime.

The Changing Social Tapestry in Post–Civil War Lebanon

Over the past few decades the social tapestry in Lebanon has changed in ways that help explain why sectarianism has kept a stubborn grip on the country, why Hezbollah has suc-ceeded so well in mobilizing support, and why inter-confes-sional cooperation is more elusive today than it was a few decades ago. The key changes were a result of Lebanon's terrible civil war, which claimed nearly 150,000 lives, or nearly 5 percent of the country's population.

It is commonly assumed that the fifteen-year civil war in Lebanon, ending in 1990, was a conflict only between Christians and Muslims. There is some truth to this, for the main line of battle, especially in the first years of the con-flict, divided the politically dominant Christian Maronite community and the mainly Muslim Palestinian resistance movement, which saw Lebanon as a battleground in their war to wrest a homeland from Israel. However, this notion obscures much more complex patterns of belligerence in-volving many different sectarian groups at odds over the Palestinian cause. Many Lebanese Christians, especially the Greek Orthodox who accounted for about 10 percent of the population during the civil war, tended to be much more sympathetic than the Maronites to the Palestinians. The non-Arab Armenian community, which is wholly Chris-

tian, mostly stayed out of the civil war, with notable exceptions of Armenian groups fighting on both sides. The main
pro-Palestinian grouping of Lebanese during the civil war
was the Lebanese National Movement, an admixture of
Arab nationalists, communists in several flavors, and various
sectarian militias, notably from the Druze community,
which accounted for about 7 percent of the total population.
Most of the Shiʿa backed the Palestinian militias, but
smaller yet not insignificant numbers joined the Maronite
militias. Later in the war, especially in the 1980s, groups
with a distinctly Shiʿi sectarian orientation—particularly
Amal and Hezbollah—emerged as significant players. As already noted, Amal opposed the Palestinian guerrillas and
Hezbollah supported them.

Most Lebanese and others who witnessed the civil war
agree that taʾifiyya (sectarianism, or "confessionalism") became more pronounced after the civil war than during the
war. At least four factors may explain this heightened sectarianism, which have been analyzed incisively by the Lebanese sociologist Salim Nasr (S. Nasr 2003).

For one, the outbreak of intercommunal violence at the
start of the civil war forced a significant displacement of
people that transformed the previous, socially heteroge-
neous communities into more segmented patterns of living.
An unfortunate example is the well-known shopping district in West Beirut, al-Hamrah, where Christians and Muslims had lived closely together in adjacent apartments before the civil war, but today the Christian population has
shrunk and Hamrah is now predominantly Sunni Muslim.
Some observers claim that the ambience of the once cosmopolitan Hamrah has suffered as a result of this change. A
short visit to Hamrah will confirm this impression: If you
stand, at ten or eleven in the evening, outside a movie the-

ater that was once packed with patrons, today you will see only a handful of movie-goers trickle into the street when the movie ends.

Second, sectarianism has been abetted by growing economic difficulties, income inequality, and immense corruption, estimated by a UN-commissioned study, in the 1990s, to exceed $1.5 billion a year (*Daily Star*, January 20, 2001). Even before the Israeli-Hezbollah war of 2006, the country's national debt stood at $40 billion—the highest per capita national debt in the world—which had been created by massive public spending on infrastructure damaged during the civil conflicts and the Israeli invasion. (Much of the rebuilt infrastructure was destroyed by Israeli bombs in the summer of 2006, which will only add to the national debt problem.) The huge debt constrains the ability of the state to intervene in the economy and inhibits private sector investment, severely limiting economic opportunities. This has resulted in a shrinking middle class, increased flight of Lebanese with the financial means to emigrate (largely Christians, who have comparatively easier access to visas to the West), and growing dependence of the remaining population on the patronage dispensed by the new sectarian political bosses (*zuʿama*), such as Amal leader Nabih Berri, who gained immense power and personal wealth by dispensing largesse, jobs, and political favors.

A third cause of rising sectarianism concerns the revival of religious institutions and leaders, as illustrated by the strong influence of the Maronite Patriarch Mar Nasrallah Sfeir, the Sunni Grand Mufti Muhammad Rashid Qabbani, and the head of the Supreme Islamic Shiʿi Council Shaikh ʿAbd al-Amr Qabalan. Within sectarian organizations, clerics have come to predominate. In Hezbollah, for example, Muhammad Raʿad and Muhammad Fneish, the only two non-clerical members of the seven-member al-Shura ("consultation" body), the highest decision-making body in the party, were replaced by clerics in 2001. Ra'ad and Fneish, perhaps not coincidentally, were known to be pragmatists who were skeptical of the organization's belligerent risk-taking. (The only non-clerical member of al-Shura is now al-Hajj Hasan Khalil, a close adviser to Nasrallah.) Although this religious revival cannot be traced to any single factor, Syria's domination of Lebanon's political space cannot be underestimated as a key element. Syrian hegemony has stunted the growth of independent political personalities and, conversely, has fostered the promotion of pro-Syrian sycophants. A political environment with little opportunity for men and women of real stature to develop as political leaders attracts religious figures prepared to criticize widespread corruption and a generally compromised political system, and also advance a convincing normative model for a religiously rooted society.

A final reason concerns regional developments that have affected Sunni-Shiʿi relations throughout the Middle East and beyond. The political ascendancy of the majority Shiʿi community in Iraq in the wake of the American occupation has heightened the shared identity of Lebanese Shiʿa to their religious brethren in Iraq. The rise of violent Sunni movements, such as al-Qaeda's branch in Iraq, which are virulently anti-Shiʿi and frequently deny that the Shiʿa qualify as Muslims, has encouraged Shiʿi Muslims across the Middle East and even in Pakistan to identify themselves more in sectarian than secular terms. Younger Shiʿa in the region are much less likely than their fathers and grandfathers were a generation or more ago to join secular parties of the ideological left or right.

Chapter 6

Lebanon's Love-Hate Relationship with
Rafiq Hariri, and His Assassination

When Rafiq Hariri was maneuvered out of office in 1998 after six years as Lebanon's prime minister, many Lebanese were happy to see him go. They were equally happy to see him return as prime minister in 2000, however, when the Lebanese surprised even themselves by upsetting Syria's plans for fraudulent elections that would install pro-Syrian officials. Disappointment with the government of Salim al-Huss, the Sunni politician who was prime minister from 1998 to 2000, was rampant, largely because it could not cope with the economic mess that al-Hariri had bequeathed. The transparent subservience of the al-Huss government toward Syria did not help either.

In the run-up to the 2000 national elections, al-Hariri's shadow loomed very large. The publicity-shy general Ghazi Kanaan, then the Syrian pro-consul in Lebanon, dictated the redrawing of electoral districts in Beirut to facilitate simultaneous victories for Tamam Salaam, son of a former prime minister, Prime Minister al-Huss and for Rafiq al-Hariri. According to Syria's master plan, the nineteen seats in Beirut would be divided between three pliant Sunni politicians in the capital. The smart money was betting that Najib Mikati from Tripoli, known for his close ties to Syria, would head the new government. The election confounded the game-plan. Al-Hariri proved to be a steamroller. He captured eighteen seats in Beirut and vanquished his two major Sunni opponents. The nineteenth seat was left open for a Shi'i Muslim from Hezbollah. Hariri himself won his Beirut constituency with more votes than any of the other Sunni candidates in Beirut.

Hariri had been careful to cultivate good ties in Syria, including Vice President ʿAbdul Halim Khaddam, who long handled the Lebanon portfolio until Syrian leader Hafiz al-Asad passed it on to his son, Bashar. Press reports indicated a momentary warming with Bashar, to whom al-Hariri promised $400 million in foreign investment for Syria, but the rapprochement was not destined to last.

The ensuing four years, until al-Hariri's resignation in October 2004, were marked by deadlock, political frustration, and mutual animosity between al-Hariri and Emile Lahoud, Lebanon's president since 1998. Lahoud, who was widely understood to be Bashar al-Asad's *wakil* (or "deputy") and who did not hesitate to wield the considerable power of his Syrian patron, succeeded in usurping the prerogatives of his adversary. For instance, although the prime minister chairs cabinet meetings under the terms of the 1989 Ta'if accord, President Lahoud assumed the prerogative to do so. Lahoud often summarily dismissed al-Hariri's agenda for cabinet meetings.

According to the Lebanese constitution, presidents may not succeed themselves. Al-Hariri made no secret of his unhappiness with Syria's plans to extend President Lahoud's six-year term in 2004 for a further three years. Syrian president al-Asad reacted sharply, informing al-Hariri in a curt ten-minute meeting in Damascus, in August 2004, that opposing Lahoud's extension would be considered tantamount to opposing the Syrian president. Accounts of this terse encounter began ricocheting around Beirut that same evening, when the former prime minister, Salim al-Huss, stated the bottom line succinctly when he met this author: "It is done."

Syria's engineering of Lahoud's three-year extension as president was received with approval, resignation, or resentment depending on where one sat on the political spectrum. For Hezbollah, Lahoud is an ally and a guarantor that the "resistance" will not be forced to disarm. In many quarters, including among veteran politicians such al-Huss, the extension was merely another example of Syria's controlling hand in Lebanese politics. In contrast, for many Christians and Druze, and certainly for al-Hariri and his allies, Syria's diktat provoked resentment and a mood of opposition. By deploying its power so brazenly, Damascus overreached and provoked an international response. The U.S. and France acted in concert with UN Security Council Resolution 1559, passed with their joint sponsorship in September 2004, which called for the withdrawal of Syrian forces and the disarming of Hezbollah. Given al-Hariri's close relationship with President Jacques Chirac, there was much speculation about Hariri's role in crafting, or at least promoting, the resolution.

As a direct result of the extension of Lahoud, political opposition to Syrian political domination began to coalesce, particularly around Walid Jumblatt, leader of Lebanon's two hundred thousand Druze. Jumblatt organized a series of opposition meetings in the fall of 2004 at Beirut's fashionable Bristol Hotel. Prime Minister Hariri did not attend, but he was widely known to have sent friends and proxies. The October 2004 attempt on the life of Jumblatt ally Marwan Hamade, one of twenty-nine deputies who voted against the extension, was universally understood as a warning to al-Hariri in particular, and to the opposition in general.

The opposition's defiance of Syria, in the face of Damascus's warnings, gained momentum that autumn, and al-Hariri was widely understood to be the opposition's de facto leader. He was feeling sufficiently confident in January 2005 to tell Rustum Ghazali, Syria's pro-consul in Beirut from 2002 to 2005, that he would not accept any Syrian-imposed candidates on his list in the elections scheduled for May 2005. Rustum replied icily, "You have to think about it, and we have to think about it" (*New York Times,* March 22, 2005).

Rafiq al-Hariri's assassination by a car bomb explosion in Beirut, on February 14, 2005, should be understood in the context of his status as the focus of Lebanese opposition to Syrian authority. Although the assassins have not yet been conclusively identified and a UN investigation into the murder continues, there is little doubt that pro-Syrian political figures in Lebanon and their Syrian allies understood al-Hariri to be a serious threat to their political survival.

Syria, which held the political controls until its forces withdrew from Lebanon in April 2005, played a balance of power game in Lebanon and often promoted intra- and inter-sectarian divisions. The prospect of an organized coalition empowered to challenge Syrian authority would be ipso facto a hostile act toward Syria. Syria's stakes in Lebanon extended well beyond security: Syrian officials were deeply enmeshed in networks of political corruption, smuggling, and crime, and were sensitive to developments that would jeopardize its Lebanese golden goose. In 2000 President Lahoud, abruptly called off an anti-corruption drive when it seemed to threaten Syria's friends (Gambill 2006a). When Prime Minister al-Hariri, in August 1997, asked this author for an appraisal of developments in Lebanon, and I cited the rampant corruption, he replied, "Some of the people in my cabinet are criminals and should be in jail, but I can't do anything about it." His claim of impotence, although transparently self-serving, also reflected his inability to defy Syria.

The initial wave of demonstrations following the death of al-Hariri and twenty-two others traveling in his entourage was met with celebratory chest-thumping and self-congratulation in Washington, where government officials anticipated the definitive overthrow of Syrian influence by a pro-American, democratic "Cedar Revolution." But within a few weeks the situation in Lebanon became much more complex when Hezbollah regained the initiative. Hezbollah expressed gratitude to Syria with a massive demonstration of Shiʿi Muslims in Beirut on March 8, 2006, attended by some four hundred thousand people, according to journalists' estimates. Clearly many Lebanese do not object to Syrian hegemony. Indeed, Syria's influence over the country remains pervasive through its strategic coordination with Hezbollah and a coterie of pliant allies, including President Lahoud, Speaker Nabih Berri, and other major political figures such as former prime minister ʿUmar Karami from Tripoli, in northern Lebanon where pro-Syrian sentiment is notable.

In response to the Hezbollah demonstration, and to mark the one-month anniversary of al-Hariri's assassination, the Cedar Revolutionaries organized a massive rally of their own in central Beirut, on March 14, attended by as many as a million people, according to widely shared estimates—incredibly, a full quarter of the country's population. Although the rally centered on Martyr's Square, where the Ottoman governor had hanged Lebanese nationalists nearly ninety years before, the city spilled over with the sea of demonstrators. There had not been a rally of similar scale in the Middle East since four million Egyptians turned out to bury their national singer, ʿUmm Kathoum, in 1975 (al-Ahram, February 6, 1975, 1). But that massive public gathering was in a country with ten times the population of today's Lebanon. The month of dueling mass demonstrations ended with mutual recognition that neither side would prevail and that a compromise was necessary.

A wildcard player in this volatile game was the former commander-in-chief of the Lebanese army, General Michel

Aoun, a Maronite who had been in exile in France since the early 1990s and returned to Lebanon in time for parliamentary elections scheduled for May 2005. Aoun showed a penchant for overplaying his hand; he had blundered badly in Lebanese politics in the late 1980s by failing to reach out to the Shi'i, Sunni, and Druze communities, and instead launching terrible violence against his own citizens. He then recklessly challenged the Syrian Baathist regime in a "war of liberation" that had neither the support of key external or internal Lebanese players nor the means to succeed. In the process, Aoun alienated potential supporters in both Washington and his own country. Thus isolated, Aoun was forced into exile by Syria in 1990.

Aoun sustained a broad popular following in Lebanon during his exile years in France, especially among secular Christians but among the Muslim communities as well. He has been admired for his courage, honesty, and nationalism. When he returned to Lebanon, in May 2005, shortly before the scheduled parliamentary elections, established politicians viewed him with trepidation because his populist following was seen as a potential threat. Aoun joined Nabih Berri and Hezbollah in calling for a delay in the election in order to revise the electoral law, which had been designed by Syria to insure that friendly politicians would be elected and to minimize opportunities for independent candidates to emerge, especially in the Christian community. Although Aoun's supporters comprised a significant proportion of the March 14 demonstration, and they certainly expected to see Aoun emerge as a major figure in any new government, it was all too clear that Aoun's Christian rivals had no intention of inviting him to join the government and thereby improve his odds for becoming president in 2007. Aoun found allies instead within the pro-Syrian "March 8 Group" (so named after the Hezbollah-organized mass demonstration of Shi°a on that date). They calculated that buying time might lead to splits in the rival "Cedar Revolution." Under U.S. pressure, the elections were held as scheduled and were won by the anti-Syrian coalition. Ironically, the victors came to power by means of the very electoral system designed to preserve Syrian authority in Lebanon.

The May 2005 election produced three distinct blocs of votes. The Cedar Revolution, under the leadership of Saad el-Din al-Hariri, a son of the assassinated former prime minister, captured seventy-two seats, short of the two-thirds total needed to unseat the pro-Syrian president Lahoud. Amal and Hezbollah offered shared tickets and won thirty-five seats, whereas Michel Aoun aligned with pro-Syrian Christians in the North and sustained his important populist base in the Christian heartland, winning twenty-one seats. Aoun, having reasoned that his prior opposition to Syrian influence in Lebanon had been overtaken by events, counted on his new pro-Syrian stance to help forge an alliance with Hezbollah. This was consummated in February 2006, when the Aoun faction and Hezbollah signed a political pact pledging to work together to fight against corruption and for electoral and economic reform. It is significant that Hezbollah won Aoun's recognition as a legitimate party of national resistance, and held his support throughout the 2006 war and its aftermath. The new Hezbollah-Aoun coalition was in force in subsequent student elections in the universities, where Hezbollah supporters joined Aoun partisans to elect pro-Aoun candidates.

The UN investigation of al-Hariri's killing remains a major preoccupation in Lebanon and a threat to the credibility and perhaps the survival of the Syrian regime, especially if President Bashar al-Asad is directly implicated. In

August 2005, under orders from the first UN investigator Detlev Mehlis, four powerful heads of the Lebanese intelligence and state police organizations were arrested, including General Jamil al-Sayyid, previously a man of enormous power who headed al-Amn al-ᶜAmm (the General Security Directorate), often said to be the most fearsome intelligence agent in the country. The investigation was digging into the very quick of Syrian influence in Lebanon. The dangers to Lebanese who pointed fingers at Syria were real and potentially lethal as underlined by a series of explosions, assassinations, and attempted assassinations all targeting anti-Syrian personalities who had accused Syria of complicity in al-Hariri's murder. Following the killing of former prime minister al-Hariri, three leading public figures were blown up, including George Hawi, an aged leader of the Communist Party; Samir Kassir, a respected *an-Nahar* columnist; and Gibran Tueni, the an-Nahar publisher whose own columns passionately criticized Syria and Hezbollah. Tueni was killed by a massive car bomb, only hours after he returned to Beirut from his Paris home.

Hezbollah, which holds two cabinet posts in the government, has attempted to constrain the investigation by insisting that the Lebanese government maintain strict control of any tribunals operating in conjunction with it. When a majority of the Lebanese parliament passed a motion, in December 2005, to authorize a mixed Lebanon-international tribunal, Hezbollah and Amal walked out of the cabinet, accused the body of being a "tyranny of the majority," and insisted that all future action regarding the al Hariri investigation proceed according to strict consensus. Hezbollah's tactic froze the government for two months, until it was persuaded to return to the cabinet by Prime Minister Fouad Siniora. In return for Hezbollah's renewed participation in the government, Siniora agreed never to refer to the organization as a "militia" but only as a "national resistance group," thus effectively removing Hezbollah from being subjected to UN Security Council Resolution 1559, calling for the withdrawal of Syrian forces and the disarming of all militias in the country.

Setting the Stage for War

In the months before the summer of 2006 Beirut was preparing for a record summer tourist business. Unlike other popular Mediterranean destinations that feature package tours at cut-rate prices, Beirut's hotel owners have generally been unwilling to offer bargains to "low-end" customers, instead targeting the more affluent tourists. After the 9/11 al-Qaeda attacks in 2001, the industry had great success attracting well-to-do Arab customers who were put off by heightened border security at American and other Western destinations. Beirut became a convenient and more culturally familiar playground. Wealthy visitors flocked to villas with signature red-tile roofs, apartments, hotels, and inns in mountainous villages, less than an hour from Beirut, and came down to the capitol city to dine and play. Clearly Lebanon had recovered from the stigma of civil war and was back as a high-end tourist destination. Lebanese officials and politicians wanted to keep it that way, and Hezbollah insisted, publicly and repeatedly, that it would do nothing to jeopardize the bountiful summer trade.

Many of these same politicians were urging Hezbollah to disarm, especially after Syria pulled out its troops in April 2005. The group steadfastly refused, arguing that its armed wing was needed more than ever as the only credible force available to defend the country against an Israeli invasion.

Hezbollah's position retains strong support in the South, but there are many detractors in the country as well. In the weeks before the outbreak of open hostilities with Israel in the summer of 2006, popular skepticism of Hezbollah's refusal to disarm turned to mockery, most notably in the June 1, 2006, television broadcast of a comedy program, where an actor in the role of a *sayyid* (a descendant of the prophet Muhammad), and looking very much like a younger Hasan Nasrallah, held forth on a variety of preposterous reasons why Hezbollah would not give up its weapons. Within hours, tens of thousands of Hezbollah sympathizers demonstrated around the country to protest the disrespect implied for Sayyid Hasan. The incident clearly revealed the exposed nerves of the Shi'i community, where memories of marginalization and second-class citizenship remain vivid. Nasrallah, for his part, did not hide his pique. The incident whetted Hezbollah's appetite for a dramatic coup de théâtre directed at its arch enemy that would allow the organization to reclaim its honor and make its militia appear all the more essential.

On the Israeli side, the desire within the country's political and military leadership to have it out with Hezbollah increased markedly in 2005 and early 2006. Israeli officials have endured Hezbollah's taunting ever since their unilateral withdrawal from southern Lebanon in 2000, and have found Nasrallah's May 2000 comparison of Israel with a fragile "spider's web" especially grating. The last straw for Israeli officials seems to have been a series of secretly monitored communications between Hezbollah and Hamas, the Palestinian Islamist group, in the spring and early summer of 2006. In these exchanges the Hezbollah leadership urged the Palestinians to hang tough in negotiations with Israel over the return of an Israeli soldier captured in June 2006.

In these same exchanges Nasrallah referred to Israeli Prime Minister Yossi Olmert and Defense Minister Amir Peretz as weak (Hersh 2006, 30). When these communications came to light within Israeli leadership circles, along with reports by respected analysts that Hezbollah was developing a "first-strike" capacity to unleash massive, preemptive rocket attacks on Israel (Gambill 2006b, 2), the Israelis were less inclined to respect the rules of the game with Hezbollah that had been respected after the 2000 withdrawal. Investigative reporter Seymour Hersh refers to a meeting in the early summer of 2006 in Washington in which U.S. and Israeli officials made plans for a crushing attack on Hezbollah (Hersh 2006). It is unclear how much operational coordination took place at this meeting, if any, but there is little doubt that officials on both sides found the prospect of inflicting a devastating blow on Hezbollah very appetizing.

Tensions between Israel and Hezbollah had, in fact, been growing for months before the start of large-scale hostilities on July 12, 2006. In November 2005 Hezbollah tried to capture several Israeli soldiers in the border village of Ghajar, which sits astride the Lebanese border with the Israeli-occupied Golan Heights. The operation, thwarted by the Israeli army, represented Hezbollah's attempt to redeem its *wa'd al-sadiq* ("faithful promise") to secure the release of Lebanese prisoners in Israeli jails, including Samir Kuntar, one of the terrorists responsible for a 1979 attack in Nahariya, Israel, that killed four members of an Israeli family. Israel has steadfastly refused to release him.

In late May 2006 Hezbollah fired on an Israeli border post, wounding an Israeli soldier. A typical response to such an incident—according to the "rules of the game" developed between the two sides over the years since the Israeli withdrawn of 2000—would have the Israeli army shelling a few

Hezbollah positions and command and control centers. In this instance, however, Israel opted for a more robust response, shelling twenty Hezbollah positions along the border and destroying many of them. Hezbollah responded by upping the ante still further by launching eight Katyusha rockets at Safad, the location of the Israeli army's northern headquarters. Five of these notoriously inaccurate rockets actually hit an antennae farm near the headquarters and sent a clear reminder to Israel of the nature of Hezbollah's arsenal, which was reported to include at least twelve thousand rockets—mostly short-range Katyushas but also various longer-range rockets, notably the Iranian-supplied Zelzal-2 with a range of up to 210 kilometers. Both sides were clearly itching for a fight.

The Start of Hostilities, July 2006

Hezbollah's dramatic operation of July 12, 2006, was yet another attempt to deliver on its *wa'd al-sadiq*, but launching the attack on Israeli soil was also intended to demonstrate the organization's formidable offensive abilities and its tenacity, while at the same time appealing to Lebanese critics of the organization who had been calling on it to disarm. From a tactical standpoint, the operation was a stunning success. Hezbollah militants ambushed a motorized Israeli patrol in an unpopulated area of northern Israel on its border with Lebanon, capturing two Israeli soldiers and killing three others. After the Israeli Defense Forces pursued the militants into Lebanon on a rescue mission, five more soldiers were killed and a state-of-the-art Merkava tank destroyed.

Hezbollah's leadership group had clearly stretched the rules of the game by conducting the daring raid on Israeli soil. Although it anticipated Israeli retaliation, the leader-

135

ship expected to be able to ride it out. Initially Hezbollah's goal seemed to have been achieved to perfection. The response to Hezbollah's *wa'd al-dhakar* ("promise remembered") in *al-dahiyya* of Beirut was jubilant. But as Hezbollah's Lebanese critics would soon point out, and as Nasrallah himself would later admit, Hezbollah had made a major miscalculation.

By July 13 Israel began its retaliatory offensive against Hezbollah, and it soon became clear that the assault went well beyond what Nasrallah and company anticipated. Within a day Lebanon was blockaded from the sea, and the Beirut airport was hit, effectively closing it. Shortly after Nasrallah's offices were bombed on July 14, Hezbollah released a recorded statement from Nasrallah that was far from conciliatory: "You wanted an open war, and we are heading for an open war. We are ready for it." (Nasrallah invited listeners to look to the sea, and with perfect theatrical timing an explosion on the horizon rocked the *INS Hanit*, an Israeli naval vessel that was hit by an Iranian-produced C-802 Noor guided missile. The ship was disabled and four of its sailors killed. This was an early hint that Hezbollah might have been better prepared than Israel presumed.

With the initial outbreak of open hostilities, Israel enjoyed broad international support and Hezbollah attracted widespread international condemnation for violating Israeli territory and snatching the soldiers. Israel's unilateral withdrawal from Lebanon six years earlier allowed it some moral superiority on this score. Strong U.S. support was, of course, expected and instantly evident. Less predictable was the quick disapproval of Hezbollah's action voiced by key Arab states, including Saudi Arabia. The Saudi government criticized Hezbollah's "uncalculated adventures" (*al-Watan*, July

14, 2006), and Jordan, Egypt, and the United Arab Emirates followed suit. This coalition between the Americans and the Arab states was held together by convergent interests. The Sunni Arab governments were understandably apprehensive about the rising profile of the Shi'ite power Iran in the Arab world, the emergence of a Shi'i-dominated government in American-occupied Iraq, and the influence of Hezbollah in Lebanon. All these forces might well inspire domestic opposition forces in their own countries, especially as Hezbollah gained enthusiastic support even among the vast Sunni population of the Arab world. In the same vein, America and its Israeli ally wished to declaw Hezbollah and indeed deal a humiliating blow to an Iranian ally in Lebanon that might inspire hostile groups in Iraq.

In his first long interview after the outbreak of hostilities, on al-Jazeera television on July 21, 2006, Hezbollah leader Nasrallah referred to the widely broadcast Arab disapproval as a "surprise," and he subtly alluded to his failure to anticipate the scale of the Israeli response. As Nasrallah said, "The Israeli reaction to the capture could have been harsh but limited, were it not for the international and Arab cover."

Prosecuting the War

Israel's war plan depended heavily on its air power and on artillery bombardment from northern Israel into Lebanon. Its military objectives were to isolate the battlefield by cutting off routes of re-supply for Hezbollah, striking Hezbollah's rocket arsenal (especially its long-range rockets capable of striking far into Israel), hitting Hezbollah's command and control, and media instruments (such as the television station al-Manar), and creating a "killing box" in southern

Lebanon where Hezbollah could be destroyed in detail by bombing and shelling. These objectives allowed for Israeli strikes on roads, bridges, seaports, and airports throughout Lebanon, as well as on the densely populated *al-dahiyya*, where many of Hezbollah command and control centers were thought to be located. Israel also struck al-Manar television repeatedly throughout the war, but except for an interruption of several minutes, the station never went off the air. On July 15 Israeli bombs targeted the home of Ayatollah Fadlallah, destroying it. The bombing of this home surprised Lebanese analysts, as Fadlallah's relations with Nasrallah were known to be tense as a result of Fadlallah's criticism of Hezbollah's periodic political inflexibility.

Within days of the start of the Israeli military response, hundreds of targets had been struck across southern Lebanon, around Beirut, in the Beqaa valley, and even in northern Lebanon. The population of the South and *al-dahiyya* was forced to flee en masse to relative safety wherever it could be found, often in schools or parking garages, if not with friends and relatives. Israel's plan in establishing its "killing box" in the South was clearly to force out all civilians. To that end Israel not only struck gasoline stations and possible militia positions, but it also hit food stores, as though to ensure that the civilians could not endure a siege. Hezbollah responded by firing rockets at Israel, usually at least one hundred and fifty rockets a day, but two hundred and fifty rockets on the last day of the war. In an unprecedented response, on July 16, Hezbollah struck the city of Haifa, home to nearly 275,000 people with longer-range rockets provided by Syria and Iran. Eight people died in the first attack on Israel's third largest city. Hezbollah's Zelzal-2 rockets could strike Tel Aviv, although none were fired, and the Israeli army claims to have destroyed most of them in the first days of the war. The advantage of the short-range Katyusha is that it can be fired in about a minute, far quicker than Israeli detection equipment can find it, whereas the larger rockets require a more elaborate launcher and much more time. Facing an enemy with complete air superiority and plenty of detection capability, the larger rockets are harder to fire successfully.

The day after Haifa was hit by rocket fire, Prime Minister Olmert addressed the Knesset and stated his goals as the return of the two captured soldiers, a complete cease-fire, meaning the end of Hezbollah's presence close to Israel's border with Lebanon; the deployment of the Lebanese army in the South; and the expulsion of Hezbollah from the South. He emphasized his determination to see to the elimination of Hezbollah as a military force and to the dismantling of all Lebanese and non-Lebanese militias, as required by UN Security Council Resolution 1559. At the United Nations, Israeli Ambassador Dan Gillerman, a frequent guest on American television news programs, echoed his prime minister's sentiments by repeatedly referring to Hezbollah as a cancer that would have to be cut out. The Israelis certainly have no monopoly on this sort of language; Hezbollah propaganda routinely refers to Israel as a cancer (Qassem 2005, 15). What Gillerman and his prime minister revealed in their comments was the common expectation that Hezbollah somehow could be expunged from Lebanon. The Israelis were eager to persuade a credulous White House that this was entirely realistic. In confidential discussions with the White House, Israel promised President Bush a "quick and decisive" result (author's private sources) and reportedly told Rice: "You did it in about 70 days [in Kosovo], but we need half of that—35 days" (Hersh 2006, 31).

Israeli efforts to excise the "cancer" of Hezbollah proved as deadly as misapplied chemotherapy for a cancer patient. The turning point might have been the Israeli bombing of Qana on July 30, killing twenty-eight civilians. After this tragedy, support for Israel's campaign in the Arab capitals melted under the heat of public outrage and demonstration. For instance, in Egypt, scores of demonstrations erupted around the country in late July and August. Although none of them were massive—the largest involved eight thousand demonstrators—the widespread underlying anger and foment in response to the July war shook the Mubarak regime and prompted a reversal of tone.

Hezbollah proved more resilient than the Israeli analysts had predicted. Israeli Brigadier General Guy Zur, commander of the 162d Armored Division that fought in Lebanon, described Hezbollah as "by far the greatest guerrilla group in the world" (USA Today, September 14, 2006). After more than a month of Israeli bombardment, Hezbollah emerged with its support intact, if not bolstered, in the Shiʿi community. Its impressive and rapid response to the needs of those whose homes and lives were ravaged—mostly but not all Shiʿi Muslims—further consolidated Hezbollah's impressive base of support. Its fighters left IOUs for items taken from shops during the war. One shopkeeper from Debin, a small village in the South, reported receiving $1,000 for redeemed IOUs (Leenders 2006, 46). More important, Hezbollah paid $10,000 to $12,000 to anyone losing their home. As many as fifteen thousand homeless families received the grants. Affiliated architects and engineers planned the construction of new homes, doctors dispensed free medicine, and about twenty-five thousand free meals were distributed daily in the weeks following the cease-fire.

By the time a UN- and Lebanon-brokered cease-fire was finally in place in mid-August 2006, Israel and the United States were forced to dramatically scale back their demands and expectations for the war's outcome. Indeed, a "seven-point plan" promulgated by the Lebanese government, preserving the sovereign prerogatives of Lebanon, would decisively shape the cease-fire. The centerpiece for the ending of the war was the decision in UN Security Council Resolution 1701 to enhance an existing peacekeeping force in southern Lebanon, the UNIFIL, which was first created in 1978 to oversee an Israeli withdrawal, after its Litani Operation. With heavy European involvement, the UN force would become UNIFIL on steroids, or so the architects of Resolution 1701 hoped. In practice, however, the force is explicitly prohibited from taking any action to disarm Hezbollah without Lebanese government approval—and this is highly unlikely to be forthcoming.

Outsiders often forget that the Lebanese have suffered tremendously under Israeli attacks for three decades, and so one of UNIFIL's key tasks is to insure that Lebanese civilians are permitted to peacefully return to and rebuild their devastated villages. Given Hezbollah's broad base of support, and the fact that its Lebanese supporters see no other force that can thwart Israel should it decide to re-ignite the war, it is completely unrealistic that the new international contingents will succeed either in disarming Hezbollah or in diminishing its appeal. If UNIFIL is going to succeed, it will need the cooperation—not the animosity—of Hezbollah. For its part, Hezbollah has formally declared its agreement, with the provision that any of its members who are found carrying arms may be detained and disarmed. In effect, what is being pursued is a "don't ask, don't tell" policy. The major question is whether UNIFIL-plus will operate not only competently but fairly. The key to restoring stability to southern Lebanon is not only to see Hezbollah stand down but also for the new force to avoid being seen as an instrument of Israeli influence or occupation.

UN Resolution 1702 also provides for the deployment of the Lebanese army in force to the South, as Israel demanded, but the army has been deployed, as several of its generals noted, to work bi-ta'awun ma'a al-muqawama (in cooperation with "the resistance," meaning Hezbollah). This is not surprising, as about half the rank and file of the Lebanese army are Shi'i Muslims and the resistance is popular with the army.

The war that broke out between Israel and Hezbollah during the summer of 2006 lasted thirty-four days. During this time half the population of northern Israel was displaced (approximately 500,000 people) and southern Lebanon was largely emptied of its civilian population—900,000 people were evacuated, or nearly one-quarter of Lebanon's population. By the war's end, 43 Israeli and 1,109 Lebanese civilians had been killed. The military casualties included 118 Israeli and 28 Lebanese soldiers, and roughly 200 Hezbollah fighters. Israel claims to have killed as many as 500 Hezbollah militants in July and August of 2006, but independent and reliable sources judge this number to be too high. Material losses were considerable, totaling approximately $500 million in Israel and about $4 billion in Lebanon, which saw the undoing of fifteen years of post–civil war reconstruction. About 900 factories were hit and 1,500 homes severely damaged or destroyed.[2]

[2] See http://news.bbc.co.uk/2/hi/middle_east/5257128.stm.

Both sides paid a heavy price for the war, with Lebanon paying the heaviest by far. But it was a war without an unequivocal winner. Both Israel and Hezbollah went to war to bolster their credibility and perceived ability to deter enemies, yet in neither case did they fully succeed. Each side seriously misread its adversary. After the war of arms ended, the war of words began, as each side struggled to persuade friend and foe alike of their victory, revealing the fragility of the claims of both sides.

Conclusion

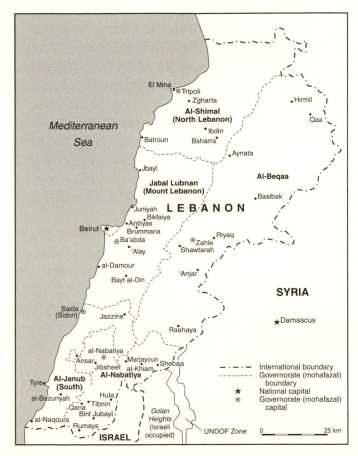

Map 2. Major cities and some important towns and villages, as well as Lebanon's five provinces (the South has sometimes been divided into two provinces: the South and al-Nabatiya).

The Islamic month of Ramadan, a time of daily fasting and reflection on the meaning of the Quran and the mercy of Allah, began in late September 2006 and concluded a month later with the traditional three-day feast. Throughout the Islamic world, families and friends gathered for the *iftar*, the breaking of the fast, at dusk. Following the meal it is customary for guests and hosts to chat about religion and the issues of the day. In many homes these discussions turn into long debates. This was certainly the case in Cairo, where the author lived during the fall of 2006 and where many *iftar* discussions focused on the July war in Lebanon. A month and a half after the August 14 cease-fire, many Egyptians were still outraged at the suffering inflicted on the Lebanese and the unwillingness of the U.S. to join international efforts aimed at an early cease-fire. In solidly middle- and upper-class Muslim homes, where secular values were often openly embraced, televisions were more commonly tuned to the BBC World Service or al-Arabiya (a less polemical rival to al-Jazeera) than to Hezbollah's al-Manar, but Hezbollah still received widespread respect, even admiration, for its success in confronting Israel.

Admiration of Hezbollah was seen not only in the homes of privileged Cairenes. Throughout Egypt in July and August there were dozens of demonstrations to protest the war or express solidarity with the Lebanese and often with Hezbollah. On August 4, 2006, for instance, demonstrations in Cairo involving about eight thousand people were timed to coincide with parallel ones in Baghdad, Amman, and Damascus. Many of the demonstrations were organized by the Society of Muslim Brothers, a venerable Egyptian Sunni Muslim group, but they were also joined by non-Islamist opposition groups including the Kefaya movement. If the demonstrations over the course of the war engaged tens of thousands of Egyptians, they were only the most obvious manifestation of a seething anger among the broader public. Egyptians talked openly about this reaction to the Lebanon war after the August cease-fire. What was most remarkable about the demonstrations in Egypt and elsewhere was that the Sunni Muslims publicly expressed solidarity for a trademark Shiʿi party. The presumed Sunni-Shiʿi sectarian divide that fascinates a variety of pundits and scholars proved to be a marginal phenomenon, whereas Hezbollah's example of resistance and its rejection of quiescence catalyzed support among many Sunni (cf. V. Nasr 2006). Muhammad Mahdi ʿAkef, the Cairo-based Supreme Guide of the Brothers, issued a strong statement in favor of Hezbollah and even promised to send ten thousand men to fight in Lebanon (although none was actually dispatched). Shaykh Yusif al-Qaradawi, the Egyptian-born Sunni cleric whose television program is seen by a vast Arab audience on al-Jazeerah, insisted on Sunni-Shiʿi cooperation, castigated the Saudi regime for its criticism of Hezbollah, and fulminated against Arab regimes in general for their weakness.

The Brothers' support illustrates precisely why ruling elites in the Islamic world find Hezbollah so worrisome, namely, that it may inspire copycat dissent movements in their own societies, especially if sectarian divisions become less salient and pan-Islamic sentiments grow. In Saudi Arabia, during the July war, in an attempt to forestall Shiʿi-Sunni solidarity, the regime reiterated the admonition of some anti-Shiʿi clerics that Saudi Muslims were not permitted to pray for Shiʿi Hezbollah.

As the war between Israel and Hezbollah continued into August 2006, swelling anger against Israel and resentment of Arab governments for accrediting Israel's offensive forced the Egyptian government to backtrack in its public statements about the conflict. President Husni Mubarak downplayed his earlier criticisms of Hezbollah and began criticizing Israel for its "disproportionate" attacks on Lebanon. A seventy-member Egyptian delegation led by the heir apparent to the presidency, Gamal Mubarak, arrived in Beirut in early August to show solidarity with Lebanon. Similar backtracking was under way in Jordan and Saudi Arabia, where, by late July, public expressions of solidarity with the Lebanese and Hezbollah were expressed by Saudi officials, albeit grudgingly. Although some ultra-conservative clerics throughout the Sunni world still refused to countenance prayers on behalf of the "heretical" Shiʿa, others were less reticent to encourage solidarity.

In Damascus, where Hezbollah's secretary-general Nasrallah was already a popular figure, the July war prompted a rush on souvenir paraphernalia, including key rings, shirts, buttons, bumper stickers, and posters featuring either Nasrallah alone or alongside Syrian president Bashar al-Asad and his father, the late Hafez al-Asad. Nasrallah was widely celebrated as a latter-day Salah al-Din (Saladin), the Kurdish general widely seen in the Arab world as a great Arab hero for his liberation of Jerusalem from the Crusaders in 1187.

Hezbollah's example of military strength against Israel also galvanized Palestinians living under Israeli occupation. As in the past, when successful resistance in southern Lebanon helped to inspire Palestinian militants to wage their own uprising against Israel, pro-Hezbollah sentiment exploded in the Palestinian territories on the West Bank and the Gaza Strip. Hezbollah posters and graffiti spread throughout the occupied territories, and Hezbollah-run al-

Manar television enjoyed a boost in Palestinian viewership, though al-Jazeera remains more popular by far. Most Palestinians were behind the Shiʿi organization despite ambivalence within the Palestinian Authority where there was concern that the Lebanese battle shifted Western media attention away from Palestinian suffering under U.S.-orchestrated sanctions. Nevertheless, Fatah president Farouk Qaddoumi, speaking to some of the more than two hundred thousand Palestinian refugees in Lebanon, embraced Hezbollah's "success" in the war (*Daily Star*, July 30, 2006). Within Palestine itself a local pop-music group, *firkat al-shimal* (the "Band of the North"), recorded a tribute to Nasrallah, "al-saqr Lubnan" (the hawk of Lebanon) that became a runaway hit in the West Bank. The lyrics celebrate "the boldness and courage that characterizes this battle [as] Islamic courage," exclaiming that the Palestinians only want a "free life" and that they welcome death in order to achieve it.[1] Concerned about the growing influence of Hezbollah within the territories, Israeli occupation forces began checking cell phones of young Palestinians and arresting those with Nasrallah screensavers.

In other Arab settings in the months following the war, CDs containing speeches by Nasrallah outsold recent recordings by popular Lebanese singers Nancy Ajram and Haifa Wahbe, and the speeches themselves influenced Arab pop culture. Nasrallah's tribute to Hezbollah fighters in the first days of the war inspired a wildly popular song by the Lebanon-based Julia Boutros entitled "Ahibaii" (My beloved ones). Its lyrics include the lines, "I want to kiss your heads and kiss your fingers on the triggers."[2]

---

[1] An MP3 version of the song is available at http://netzoo.net/the-hawk-of-lebanon/.

[2] For the lyrics, see http://www.julia.ws/.

Strong support for Hezbollah during and after the July war was also apparent within Iraq's Shi^{c}i community. The leading Shi^{c}i religious leader Ayatollah Sistani issued a *fatwa* on July 16, 2006, condemning the Israeli attack on Lebanon as disproportionate and authorizing his deputies (*wakils*) to collect alms for humanitarian assistance to the Lebanese. Since Sistani is by far the most revered cleric in Iraq (as well as a highly influential figure among Shi^{c}a in Lebanon),[3] his ruling effectively validated the shared identity of non-Lebanese Shi^{c}a with their brethren in Lebanon.

Hezbollah has also been embraced by the firebrand Iraqi Shi^{c}i cleric Muqtada al-Sadr and his loyal supporters in the impoverished suburbs of Baghdad. His scholarly credentials as a Shi^{c}i cleric are weak, but as the son of the revered Ayatollah Muhammad al-Sadr (assassinated in 1999, reputedly under orders from Saddam Hussein), Muqtada has inherited his father's broad social support base among what his relative Musa al-Sadr referred to a generation ago in Lebanon as the *al-mahrumin* (the deprived). On August 4, 2006, Muqtada led a demonstration in Baghdad that included about one hundred thousand of his followers who chanted "death to Israel," as Muqtada railed against what he called *al-muthalath al-mash'um* ("the evil triangle"), presumably a jibe at George W. Bush's "Axis of Evil" and a reference to the United States, Israel, and the Arab states supporting Israel's campaign in Lebanon

[3] Precise figures on those who follow or "imitate" (*taqlid*) Sistani in Lebanon are not available, but he certainly enjoys a broader following than Lebanon's widely respected Ayatollah Muhammad Hussein Fadlallah, or even the Iranian supreme leader Ayatollah Ali Khamenei, whom Hezbollah considers the official source for Islamic law. This author's impression, based on informal interviews and discussion with a wide variety of Lebanese Shi^{c}a, is that, as of November 2006, at least 60 percent of all Lebanese follow Sistani, with the rest following Fadlallah. Very few consider themselves "imitators" of Khamenei.

Hezbollah in a Fractured Postwar Lebanon

In contrast to the celebrations of Hezbollah's "victory" in the wider Arab world, within Lebanon adulation of Hezbollah was far from universal. Although the organization benefited from pan-Lebanese expressions of solidarity and anti-Israel feeling during the armed conflict and in the weeks after the cease-fire, cross-confessional solidarity faded quickly as Lebanese began to openly question Hezbollah's role in provoking the war. It was hard to celebrate a "victory" in the face of a reconstruction bill now estimated at $4 billion. The war has been an economic calamity for the country. It will take at least two years to complete most of the infrastructure repairs, which includes the rebuilding of some seventy-eight bridges. The war sabotaged the tourist season of 2006, representing, according to reliable estimates, a loss of $2 billion in income. Future tourism is likely to suffer as travelers weigh the risks of a visit to Lebanon against other, less conflict-prone locales. And further mitigating any sense of triumph was the human cost of the war— 1,109 dead civilians and 15,000 displaced families whose homes were destroyed or badly damaged.

The recent war has, in fact, split Lebanon in two. One Lebanon is represented by a coalition of mainly Sunnis, Druze, and Christians that coalesced following the assassination of the former prime minister and Sunni Muslim Rafiq al-Hariri. This is the so-called Cedar Revolution that united in reaction to Hariri's murder to demand a full investigation into the assassination, and to call on Syrian forces to leave Lebanon. This group, which won the 2005 parliamentary elections by capturing 72 of 128 seats, was in power during the 2006 war. Many of its members consider Hezbollah's provocative actions, including the July 12 ambush in

Israel, as a "coup d'état." They accuse the Shiʿi group of being an agent of Syria and Iran, with the ultimate aim of installing a theocratic Islamic Republic on the shores of the Mediterranean.

The other Lebanon is also a coalition, consisting of much of the Shiʿi community and large elements of the Christian community—especially the many followers of the magnetic Maronite politician and former general Michel Aoun. This coalition is somewhat confusingly called the March 8 Group, in commemoration of the large demonstration led by Hezbollah and Amal on March 8, 2005, ostensibly to respect Hariri's memory but also to thank Syria for its supposed role in maintaining peace in the country. In fact, the Aounists, probably comprised close to half of the one million people who participated in the massive March 14, 2005, demonstration that made the Cedar Revolution a phenomenon known 'round the world. When their leader, General Aoun, was shut out of the government after the 2005 elections, they shifted to the opposition. Since then, Aoun's Free Political Movement has shown considerable strength in university-student elections, and in the important professional associations of lawyers, doctors, and engineers. The "Aounists" and the Shiʿa share a profound sense of victimization in the face of what they see as a corrupt and unresponsive political system. They work together to expand their share of power in significant measure at the expense of the Sunni Muslims.

Timur Goksel, a Turk who served for twenty-five years as political adviser to UNIFIL and who is respected for his sage reflections on Lebanese politics, observed:

> Now that the war is over, any hope for a true national unity in Lebanon has again become a dream. Nasrallah's repeated calls for a strong central state free of corruption, and able to

protect Lebanon, as a prerequisite for his party to give up its weapons usually generates knowing smiles from those who believe that Lebanon's "tribalism" is not going to change any time soon. The Maronite–Sunni–Druze coalition that is the majority in the parliament has a single priority now: to stop Hezbollah from using its arms and recently enhanced political standing from changing the sectarian system's domestic political and economic balances.[4]

Hezbollah, meanwhile, rejects blame for precipitating the July 2006 war. Nasrallah claims that Israel had been preparing an attack on Hezbollah even months before the capture of the Israeli soldiers on July 12, 2006. Israel, it is alleged, used the capture as a convenient pretext to launch its failed campaign of annihilation. In a remarkable interview on Lebanese television, on August 27, 2006, however, Nasrallah took a very different tack and conceded that his organization had miscalculated: "If any of us [on the fifteen-member political-military council] had a 1 percent concern that Israel was going to reply in this savage manner we would not have captured those soldiers." At the same time Hezbollah accused the ruling coalition of complicity in an American- and Israeli-led plot to destroy the organization.

Nasrallah used this same television interview to attempt to reassure his fellow Lebanese that Hezbollah's weapons were only for fighting the Israeli enemy and would not be "pointed" at fellow Lebanese. These words were coupled, however, with a demand for a "national unity" government that would include representatives of the political party of Hezbollah's main Christian ally, Michel Aoun. His opponents were not reassured, claiming that the insistence on a

[4] Interview by Internet, October 8, 2006.

national unity parliamentary coalition run by strict consensus—thus granting Hezbollah veto power—was tantamount
to bullying the current government out of existence. Prime
Minister Fouad Siniora and his coalition partners further
accuse Nasrallah of serving Syria's interests by precipitating
a political crisis, thereby disrupting the efforts of the present
Lebanese government to authorize an international tribunal
to try suspects in the killing of former prime minister Hariri.

Both sides dug in their heels as the political stakes of the
showdown are, in fact, high. Hezbollah is using its arms and
enhanced political standing in the Islamic world to attempt
to change the delicate political balance of Lebanon's sectarian government in its favor. And the ruling Maronite-
Sunni-Druze coalition is doing what it can to block such
change. The veteran political observer Sofia Saadeh puts
the dilemma quite clearly:

> When there is a demographic change in this country . . . the
> constitution does not explain how this can be translated at
> the level of politics. Since the Lebanese system revolves
> around the sects sharing power, this is a very crucial short-
> coming. So, every time a sect wants to move forward and
> upward in the political hierarchy, we end up with strife. In a
> regular democracy, the votes will tell you which direction
> to take. Unfortunately, in Lebanon, there is no such mecha-
> nism. The ascendancy of the Shi'i is being fought by
> the Sunnis.[5]

The fall of 2006 was marked by an escalation of tension
and demands. On October 31 Nasrallah's call for a national
unity government turned into a blatant ultimatum: the government must either agree to a new consensus arrangement,

[5] Interview by author, November 13, 2006, Beirut.

with a Hezbollah veto over all government measures, or face widespread demonstrations and other forms of organized pressure such as blocking the route to the national airport. Following the resignation of an allied Sunni member, and in conjunction with these demands, all five Shiʿi members of the government resigned from the cabinet, leaving even the legal status of the rump government in question. Because the al-Taʾif agreement, which ended the civil war in 1989, required every major sect to participate in government, the departure of the Shiʿa prompted the pro-Hezbollah president Lahoud to assert that the government was no longer legitimate and could not undertake major initiatives—including the seating of an international tribunal.

The postwar crisis took a deadly turn on November 21, 2006, with the assassination of thirty-three-year-old Pierre Gemayel, the Lebanese Minister of Industry. The slain minister was the son of Amin Gemayel, a former president, and grandson and namesake of the founder of the Phalange militia, the largest Christian-led militia during the civil war. The victim had frequently criticized Hezbollah and Syria, and was the fifth and most recent prominent critic of Syrian involvement in Lebanon who was assassinated since 2005. Many fingers understandably pointed at Syria, which has demonstrated a penchant for eradicating its Lebanese adversaries. This time, however, some informed observers were skeptical about Syria's culpability, especially as reports surfaced suggesting that Gemayel held confidential talks with Hezbollah political ally Michel Aoun in the weeks preceding his gangland-style killing. If true, the reports imply that Lebanese rivals might have been responsible. Whoever was responsible, the killing increased fears among Lebanese that they were edging toward an eruption of wider violence. One hopeful sign was found in the wisdom of Pierre Gemayel's father, former president Amin Gemayel, who called upon the tens of thousands of mourners and supporters that gathered at Martyr's Square in Beirut to abjure revenge. Although he refused a condolence call from General Aoun, he did speak with Hasan Nasrallah—whose son, Hadi, was killed fighting Israel—and the two found common emotional ground according to press reports.

Nonetheless, the joint effort by Hezbollah, Amal, and the Aounists to topple the Siniora government picked up steam as December began with a massive peaceful protest gathering in downtown Beirut. With Prime Minister Fouad Siniora and many of his ministers hunkered down in their offices in the Grand Serail, the Ottoman-era seat of government, fearful that their offices would be occupied if they vacated, half a million Shiᶜa and Christians (with Shiᶜa predominating) vowed to stay put until the government succumbed to pressure and either accepted a national unity government or agreed to call elections. The previous year Western governments, especially the U.S. government, endorsed and encouraged similar protests to topple a pro-Syrian government, but now the shoe was on the other foot. If Washington and the predominantly Sunni world was aghast at Shiᶜi muscle flexing, especially since it might well benefit Iran's power projection into the wider Middle East, perhaps the most profound importance of the December protest, if it remains peaceful, will be as a model for collective action in other Arab locales, which is a prospect no less distressing to the Arab world's autocrats.

What Next?

Lebanon has rather stubbornly demonstrated, at many different times and under many different circumstances, that its political system is not readily dominated by any community, at least for very long. This is why half-solutions and compromise usually prevail, just as they will likely prevail in the 2006 crisis.

Much will depend on how true Hezbollah remains to the positions it has frequently espoused over the past decade and a half, particularly regarding the prospects for an Islamic state in Lebanon and the party's attachment to Lebanon as a pluralist society. Nasrallah and his colleagues have repeatedly declared that the prospects for establishing a state based on Islamic rule will probably never exist in Lebanon, as such a state could only be established on the basis of broad consent. Hezbollah, its leaders have promised, is committed to the survival of Lebanon as a diverse, multicultural society, because it is precisely Lebanon's diversity that defines its unique appeal and character. As Nasrallah told Rafiq al-Hariri in their first of several reconciliation meetings in 2000: "We don't possess second citizenship, we were born here, we will die here and we will be buried here. And we starve here and satisfy our appetite here, so nobody may outbid us on our patriotism or on [our right] to belong."[6]

The July war threw a bomb into Lebanese politics, and it was utterly predictable that the Shiʿa would emerge from the war as a mobilized, assertive, and more militant community. At the same time the fears that grip Hezbollah's opponents are rational and wholly understandable, especially given the destruction Hezbollah provoked in the July war. And it is not only fear that needs to be addressed. Contending interests must be accommodated, no easy matter even in quieter times.

Postwar reconstruction will require not only engineering prowess to rebuild scores of bridges but also the political and moral courage to build political bridges to traverse the gulf

---

[6] The author wishes to thank Ali Safa for finding Nasrallah's comment.

of anger that continues to divide the two Lebanons. It remains to be seen how the bridges of cooperation will be designed and how sturdy they will be. Collective memories of civil war are still fresh in Lebanon, and even fresher memories of violence and destruction linger, especially throughout the Shi'i community. There are, in short, strong incentives to find pragmatic compromises to avoid a further disaster in a country that has had more than its share of calamities, a country where Hezbollah is clearly fated to play a continuing and important role. And, one hopes, a constructive one.

Glossary

al-ʿAshura — literally, "the tenth"; refers to the tenth day of the Islamic month of Muharram, when the Imam Hussein, grandson of the Prophet Muhammad, was martyred at Karbala

Amal — the Shiʿi reform group founded by Musa al-Sadr; Hezbollah's main political rival in the Shiʿi community

ayatollah — literally, "sign of God"; refers to the learned Shiʿi scholars eligible to render *ijtihad*

Baʿth — literally, "renaissance"; refers to the Arab nationalist party, which has had pro-Iraq and pro-Syrian branches in Lebanon

al-dahiyya — "the suburb"; usually understood in Lebanon to refer collectively to the southern suburbs of Beirut, where the Shiʿa predominate

al-daʿwa — "the call" to Islam, a reference to the Shiʿi party (Hizb al-Daʿwa) founded in Iraq in 1958

fatwa (pl., *fatuwa*) — a religious ruling or opinion issued by a Muslim cleric

husseiniya — a building used especially during Muharram for honoring Imam Hussein and members of his extended family, including his sister Zaynab

ijtihad — a religious interpretation by a qualified Shiʿi scholar, usually an *ayatollah*

imam — the term used in Shiʿi Islam to refer to one of the twelve male successors to the Prophet, beginning with Imam ʿAli and ending with the Twelfth Imam, who is believed to be in occultation (a state of being present but unseen). Sometimes, in a Shi'i village for instance, the title *imam* simply refers to a local religious figure.

Jabal 'Amil — the venerable Shi'i heartland in southern Lebanon that extends into the southern Beqaa valley

majlis (pl., *majalis*) — literally, a place of sitting; a term often used to mean "parliament" or to refer to the gatherings of Shi'a during Muharram to reflect on the meaning of Karbala

marji' al-taqlid — literally, a "source of imitation"; a leading *mujtahid* who is considered a reliable source of *ijithad* by many Shi'a (for instance, Muhammad Hussein Fadlallah of Lebanon or 'Ali Sistani of al-Najaf, Iraq)

mujtahid — a cleric who is qualified to do *ijtihad*

al-Shari'a — Islamic law

shaykh — a term of respect, often used to refer to learned Islamic scholars

ta'ifiyya — confessionalism or sectarianism

ta'ziyah — in Lebanon, this refers to a mourning ritual (whereas in Iran it often refers to the dramatic performance of Hussein's martyrdom and events surrounding the Karbala epic)

al-timthiliyya — a performance, as in the dramatic re-creation of the tragedy of Karbala

ziyyara (pl., *ziyyarat*) — a visit to the tomb or to a site associated with one of the twelve Shi'i Imams or to other significant descendants of the prophet

za'im (pl., *zu'ama*) — political boss, usually with the connotation of a figure who dispenses patronage in exchange for support

Additional Reading

Lebanon is a complex country that observers all too quickly try to reduce to Christian-Muslim or sectarian labels, as though Lebanese fit into neat cultural boxes. Indeed, even officials who should know better are sometimes seduced by this sort of confessional typecasting, as though people's behavior is predetermined by a cultural nugget that is magically transmitted from one generation to the next. This is lazy thinking. If confession did determine behavior, the idea of a Lebanese nationality would be an illusion, civil war would be the norm, not the aberration, and Lebanon would be divided into a messy collection of emirates and enclaves. Instead, even in the early twenty-first century—when sectarian identities are peculiarly salient—we must take account of regional, class, or ideological differences, not to mention political jealousies and simple opportunism, to think sensibly about Lebanon and its politics.

For those who are provoked or curious to learn more about Lebanon and its complex history, there is probably no better starting place than Kamal Salibi's rich and elegantly written introduction to Lebanon, *A House of Many Mansions*. There are several important accounts of the incremental collapse of Lebanon into civil war in 1975, and the many internal and external dimensions of violence since then, but Elizabeth Picard's incisive *A Shattered Country* is especially sophisticated yet accessible.

In recent decades, and for that matter over the past two centuries, Lebanon has been deeply affected by external powers. Israel has played a weighty role in Lebanon's history, and never less so than the momentous 1982 invasion and its aftermath which included the rise of Hezbollah. Ze'ev Schiff and Ehud Ya'ari's *Israel's Lebanon War* is an indispensable account of a grand plan gone wrong. Daniel Sobelman's more recent *New Rules of the Game* brings to bear many Hebrew and Arabic sources, and a detailed knowledge of Lebanon, to analyze the Israeli confrontation with Hezbollah in southern Lebanon, particularly after the Israeli withdrawal in 2000.

Distant Relations, a volume edited by Houchang Chehabi, focuses on Lebanon's multifaceted connections with non-Arab Iran. The editor and the other contributors to the volume combine scholarly craftsmanship with sometimes unique insights into the five-hundred-year relationship between the two countries, as well as the role of Shiʿi religious institutions and personalities in maintaining and redefining the liaison.

Until recent years the Arab Shiʿi Muslim communities were often relegated to footnotes in scholarly publications. These communities in Lebanon, Bahrain, Iraq, Saudi Arabia, Kuwait, and elsewhere have all been experiencing what is still best called "social mobilization." The term implies the changes wrought within the various Arab Shiʿi communities by virtue of education, increased mobility, a growing awareness of momentous changes across borders through growing media access as well as through pilgrimages, and other travel experiences. Many of these aspects of change are anticipated in Fuad Khuri's brilliant *From Village to Suburb*, which focused precisely on the southern suburbs of Beirut.

A variety of sometimes overlapping and momentous events have been particularly important in shaping the political consciousness of Arab Shi'i Muslims, including the Iranian revolution of 1978–79, and the Israeli and American interventions in Lebanon. The ensuing instability and violence gave rise to a number of books, the best among them arguably Robin Wright's *Sacred Rage*. If hijacking, the taking of hostages, and terrorism understandably captured the headlines a quarter of a century ago, by the mid-1980s leading Middle East scholars began to offer more broadly contextualized accounts of *Shi'ism and Social Protest*, to cite the still rewarding 1986 book edited by Juan Cole and Nikki Keddie. Two recent volumes—both notable for their accounts of Iraq and the other Arab Gulf states—include seasoned, clearly written surveys of *The Forgotten Muslims*, in the case of the book by Graham Fuller and Rend Francke, and the quests of several Arab Shi'i communities *Reaching for Power*, to cite Yitzhak Nakash's timely book. Vali Nasr offers a wider focus in *The Shi'a Revival*, where he examines the historical subordination of Shi'i Muslims to Sunni Muslim authority, and reveals growing signs of conflict and competition between the two major Islamic sects.

To the extent that Shi'i-Sunni tensions are growing in a variety of settings, no small part has been played by the Anglo-American invasion of Iraq in 2003. Jamal Sankari's biography, *Fadlallah*, offers a finely woven account of the Shi'i milieu in Iraq, in which Lebanon's Ayatollah Muhammad Hussein Fadlallah was a notable participant. Sankari's gem of a book also offers an essential account of the Lebanese context in which the cleric maneuvered. Fadlallah has been the dominant Shi'i voice in Lebanon for more than two decades, although he may now be outstaged by Hezbollah Secretary-General Hasan Nasrallah, who has become something of a folk hero in the Arab world in recent years.

Only in the early 1980s did an extensive literature on the Shi'i community in Lebanon begin to develop. My book, *Amal and the Shi'a*, made possible by a fortuitously timed adventure in southern Lebanon as the leader of a UN peacekeeping team in 1980 and 1981, came at a time when rather one-dimensional views of Shi'i Muslims prevailed in much of the press and within the U.S. government. The volume focused on the early political mobilization of the Shi'i community by Sayyid Musa al-Sadr and the role of his Amal movement, as well as on the impact of Israeli and Palestinian actions on the radicalization of the community. Fouad Ajami, a Shi'i native of the southern Lebanese village of Arnoun and now a major public intellectual and policy advocate, crafted *The Vanished Imam*, an elegant and Conrad-esque saga of Musa al-Sadr.

Younger scholars from Lebanon later made noteworthy contributions to our knowledge of Shi'i politics in Lebanon, and especially of Hezbollah.[1] Nizar Hamzeh is a longtime student of Shi'i politics, and his *In the Path of Hizbullah* offers capable and systematic analysis. Amal Saad-Ghorayeb concentrates, in *Hizbu'llah*, on the ideological development of the Shi'i party. Her assessment is comprehensive if occasionally dense. *An Enchanted Modern* by the anthropologist Lara Deeb is a richly textured, insightful excursion into the contemporary Shi'i society in Lebanon. Deeb focuses especially on Shi'i women and how religion influences their identities. Unlike any of the other books available in English, Naim Qassem's *Hizbullah*, translated from Arabic, is by a consummate insider. Qassem is, of course, the Deputy

---

[1] Like many Arabic words, "Hezbollah" is subject to various transliterations. Here we have retained the original spelling in book titles in order to avoid confusion should readers search for a book in a library or bookstore, or merely wish to cite the title.

Secretary-General of Hezbollah, and his discussion of a number of key decisions, such as the debate over participating in Lebanese elections, is often valuable and unexpectedly frank.

Finally, thanks to the wonder of Internet publishing, a solid special issue of the *MIT Electronic Journal of Middle East Studies*, titled *The Sixth War*, appeared only a few months after the July war of 2006. The issue includes extensive analyses of Hezbollah's decision making, war fighting, and postwar political orientation.

Sources Cited

Abisaab. 2006. "The Cleric as Organic Intellectual: Revolutionary Shiʿ-ism in the Lebanese Hawzas." In *Distant Relations: Iran and Lebanon in the Last 500 Years*, ed. H. E. Chehabi. London: Centre for Lebanese Studies and I. B. Tauris.

Ajami, Fouad. 1986. *The Vanished Imam: Musa al Sadr and the Shia of Lebanon*. Ithaca, N.Y.: Cornell University Press.

Alagha, Joseph Elie. 2006. *The Shifts in Hizbullah's Ideology: Religious Ideology, Political Ideology, and Political Program*. Leiden: Amsterdam University Press.

Anderson, Jon Lee. 2006. "Letter from Beirut: The Battle for Lebanon." *New Yorker*, 34–41.

Ayoub, Mahmoud. 1978. *Redemptive Suffering in Islam: A Study of the Devotional Aspects of ʿAshuraʿ in Twelver Shiʿism*. The Hague: Mouton.

Chamie, Joseph. 1981. *Religion and Fertility: Christian-Muslim Differentials*. Cambridge: Cambridge University Press.

Chehabi, H. E., ed. 2006. *Distant Relations: Iran and Lebanon in the Last 500 Years*. London: Centre for Lebanese Studies and I. B. Tauris.

Cole, Juan I., and Nikki Keddie, eds. 1986. *Shiism and Social Protest*. New Haven: Yale University Press.

Deeb, Lara. 2006. *An Enchanted Modern: Gender and Public Piety in Shiʿi Lebanon*. Princeton, N.Y.: Princeton University Press.

el-Kak, Mona Harb. 2001. "Post-war Beirut: Resources, Negotiations, and Contestations in the Elyssar Project." In *Capital Cities: Ethnographies of Urban Governance in the Middle East*, ed. S. K. Shami. Toronto: Centre for Urban and Community Studies.

Fuller, Graham E., and Rend Rahim Francke. 1999. *The Arab Shiʿa: The Forgotten Muslims*. New York: St Martin's.

Gambill, Gary C. 2006a. "The Counter-Revolution of the Cedars." In *Mideast Monitor* 1 (2) (April–May). http://www.mideastmonitor.org/issues/0604/0604_1.htm.

———. 2006b. "Hezbollah and the Political Ecology of Postwar Lebanon." In *Mideast Monitor* 1 (3) (September–October). http://www.mideastmonitor.org/issues/0609/0609_1.htm.

Hamzeh, A. Nizar. 2004. *In the Path of Hizbullah*. Syracuse: Syracuse University Press.

Harb, Mona, and Reinoud Leenders. 2005. "Know Thy Enemy: Hizbullah, 'Terrorism', and the Politics of Perception." *Third World Quarterly* 26 (1): 173–97.

Harik, Judith Palmer. 2004. *Hezbollah: The Changing Face of Terrorism.* London: Tauris.

Hersh, Seymour M. 2006. "Annals of National Security: Watching Lebanon: Washington's Interests in Israel's War." *New Yorker*, August 21, 28–33.

Hilterman, Joost. 1996. *Civilian Pawns.* Washington, D.C.: Middle East Watch.

Hourani, Guita. 2006. *The Impact of the Summer War on Migration in Lebanon: Emigration, Remigration, Evauation.* Louaize, Lebanon: Lebanese Emigration Research Center, Notre Dame University.

International Crisis Group (ICG). 2002. "Old Games, New Rules: Conflict on the Israel-Lebanon Border." Amman and Brussels: International Crisis Group.

Khuri, Fuad I. 1975. *From Village to Suburb: Order and Change in Greater Beirut.* Chicago: University of Chicago Press.

Kramer, Martin. 1993. "Hizbullah: The Calculus of Jihad." In *Fundamentalisms and the State: Remaking Politics, Economies, and Militance,* ed. M. Marty and R. S. Appleby. Chicago: University of Chicago Press.

Leenders, Reinoud. 2006. "How the Rebel Regained His Cause & the Sixth Arab-Israeli War." *MIT Electronic Journal of Middle East Studies* 6:38–56.

Melman, Yosi. 2006. "What Will Happen Next?" *Haaretz,* July 21.

MIT Electronic Journal of Middle East Studies. 2006. "The Sixth War: Israel's Invasion of Lebanon." Vol. 6. http://web.mit.edu/cis/www/mitejmes/.

Nasr, Salim. 2003. "The New Social Map." In *Lebanon in Limbo: Postwar Society and State in an Uncertain Regional Environment,* ed. T. Hanf and N. Salam. Baden-Baden: Nomos Verlagsgesellschaft.

Nasr, Vali. 2006. *The Shi'a Revival: How Conflicts within Islam Will Shape the Future.* New York: Norton.

Norton, Augustus Richard. 1987. *Amal and the Shi'a: Struggle for the Soul of Lebanon.* Austin: University of Texas Press.

———. 1990a. "Lebanon: The Internal Conflict and the Iranian Connection." In *The Iranian Revolution: Its Global Impact,* ed. J. L. Esposito. Miami: Florida International University Press.

———. 1990b. "Religious Resurgence and Political Mobilization of the Shi'a of Lebanon," in *Religious Resurgence and Politics in the Contemporary World,* ed. Emile Sahliyeh (Albany: State University of New York Press).

————. 1993. "(In)security Zones in South Lebanon." *Journal of Palestine Studies* 23 (1):61–79.

————. 2006. "The Peacekeeping Challenge in Lebanon." *MIT Electronic Journal of Middle East Studies* 6:76–79.

Pakradouni, Karim. 1983. *La Paix Manquee*. Beirut: FMA Editions.

Peters, Emryrs. 1970. "Aspects of Rank and Status among Muslims in a Lebanese Village." In *People and Culture of the Middle East*, ed. L. E. Sweet. Garden City, N.Y.: Natural History Press.

Picard, Elizabeth. 2002. *Lebanon: A Shattered Country: Myths and Realities of the Wars in Lebanon*, revised edition. New York: Holmes & Meier.

Picco, Giandomenico. 1999. *Man without a Gun: One Diplomat's Secret Struggle to Free the Hostages, Fight Terrorism, and End a War*. New York: Random House.

Qassem, Naim. 2005. *Hizbullah: The Story from Within*. London: Saqi.

Saad-Ghorayeb, Amal. 2002. *Hizbu'llah: Politics and Religion*. London, and Sterling, Va.: Pluto Press.

Salibi, Kamal. 1988. *A House of Many Mansions: The History of Lebanon Reconsidered*. London: I. B. Tauris.

Sankari, Jamal. 2005. *Fadlallah: The Making of a Radical Shi'ite Leader*. London: Saqi.

Schiff, Ze'ev, and Ehud Ya'ari. 1984. *Israel's Lebanon War*. New York: Simon and Schuster.

Shams al-Din, Muhammad Mahdi. 1985. *The Rising of al-Husayn: Its Impact on the Consciousness of Muslim Society* [based on *Thawrat al-Husayn: Zurufuha al-Ijtimaa'iyya wa-al-Athaaruha al-Insaniyya*, 1977, 5th ed.]. Translated by I. K. A. Howard. London: The Muhammadi Trust of Great Britain and Northern Ireland.

Shatz, Adam. 2004a. "In Search of Hizballah (Part I)." *New York Review of Books*, April 29.

————. 2004b. "In Search of Hizballah (Part II)." *New York Review of Books* 51 (8).

Sobelman, Daniel. 2004. *New Rules of the Game: Israel and Hizballah after the Withdrawal from Lebanon*. Tel Aviv: Jaffee Center for Strategic Studies, Tel Aviv University.

Zisser, Eyal. 2006. "Hizballah and Israel: Strategic Threat on the Northern Border." *Israel Affairs* 12 (1): 186–206.

Index

Index

Index

Index

defining terrorism and, 75–77; Egyptian criticism of, 147–49; Gaza strip and, 93, 149–50; Golan Heights and, 82, 90–93, 116; Harb al-Tummuz (July War) and, 7; international support of, 136–37; invasion by, 22, 32–34, 71; iron fist policy of, 87; Litani Operation and, 22–23, 79–80; Operation Accountability and, 84; Operation Grapes of Wrath and, 84; Qana slaughter and, 84–85; recent hostilities and, 132–43; resentment against, 148–49; "rules of the game" and, 83–88, 134–35; withdrawal from Lebanon (2000) and, 88–93, 115–18
Israel Defense Forces (IDF), 84–88
Ivory Coast, 3, 13
Izz al-Din, Hasan, 77

Jabal ʿAmil, 51–52
Jaʿfari, 24–25, 40
Jamiʿiyyat al-Mabarrat al-Khayriya (Benevolent Charity Society), 108–9
Jaysh al-Maaahdi (Army of the Guided One), 30
al-Jazeera, 46, 93, 147–48, 150
Jerusalem Post, 116n1
Jesus Christ, 84–85
Jews, 11n1
Jibsheet, 34, 36
jihad, 38
Jihan al-Bina' Development Organization, 110
Jordan, 137, 149
al-Jumblatt, Kamal, 19

Kafr Rumann, 5
Kanaan, Ghazi, 124
van Kappen, Franklin van, 84n2
Karami, ʿUmar, 128
Karbala, 4–5, 31, 45, 52, 56, 66, 85, 105
Karine-A (ship), 93
Kathoum, ʾUmm, 128

Katyusha rockets, 84–87, 135, 149
Kefaya movement, 147
Khaddam, ʿAbdul Halim, 124–25
Khalil, Hajj Hasan, 123
Khamenei, ʿAli, 54, 78, 90, 100, 151n3
al-Khansa, al-Hajj Ahmed, 52–53
al-Khansa, Muhammad Saʾid, 104–5
al-Khiam, 115
Khomeini, Ruhollah Musavi, 31, 44–45, 50, 100
al-Khuʿi, Sayyid Abu al-Qasim, 108
khums (Ramadan gifts), 109
Khuri, Fuad, 53
killing box, 137–39
Krayem, Nayif, 118
Kurds, 78, 119
Kuwait, 12, 15, 41, 55, 75

labor: agriculture and, 13–14, 105–6; emigration and, 13–14; fighter wages and, 17–18; Palestinians and, 14; revolution of the hungry and, 105–7; social welfare and, 107–12
Lahoud, Emile, 125–30, 156
language, 3, 5, 20
Latin America, 14
League of Nations, 11. See also United Nations
Lebanese Communist Party (LCP), 15
Lebanese National Movement (LNM), 17–20, 121
Lebanese Resistance Detachments. See Amal
Lebanon: al-Bazuriya, 3–5; Beirut, 5–6, 51–52, 77; changing social structure in, 120–23; civil war in, 16, 23–24, 44, 120–21; Communist Party and, 5–6, 15, 31, 37, 80, 103, 131; confessional groups (map), 1; electoral system of, 97–98; future of, 157–59; Gulf War and, 74–75; Hariri and, 124–32; identity and, 51–58; independence of, 11; Israeli invasion of, 22, 32–34, 71; Israeli withdrawal from (2000), 88–93,

Index

Index

Index

and, 50; average family size of, 13;
clerical influence and, 39–40; expanding middle class of, 45–46; Hussein (grandson of Muhammad) and,
49–51; institutional services and,
107–12; Karbala and, 4–5; Litani
Operation and, 22; *marjiʿ al-taqlid*
and, 100; *mithaq al-watani* (national
pact) and, 12; as minority, 49; Muhammad's succession and, 49; al-
Najaf and, 4–5; parliamentary representation and, 97; patronage networks and, 14–15; politics and, 6–7,
14–18, 98–105; proxy wars and, 72–
73; rituals of, 51–58; Saddam Hussein and, 5; al-Sadr and, 18–21;
shariʿa and, 39–40; Siniora government and, 157; spread of, 51–52;
Sunni cooperation and, 148
Shultz, George, 82
al-Shura (consultation body), 123
Sierre Leone, 29
Siniora, Fouad, 131–32, 155, 157
al-Sistani, ʿAli, 31n1, 100–101, 151
SLA, 83, 88, 90
Sobelman, Daniel, 84
social welfare, 107–12
Society of Muslim Brothers, 147–48
Soleimanpour, Hade, 79
Soviet Union, 36
Stethem, Robert, 77
suicide bombers, 6, 71, 80–81, 86
Sunni Muslims, 123, 155; Aoun and,
129; Arab nationalism and, 16; average family size of, 13; clerical influ-
ence and, 40; Hussein (grandson of
Muhammad) and, 49–51; as majority, 49; *mathaq al-watani* (national
pact) and, 11–12; Muhammad's succession and, 49; Shiʿi cooperation
and, 148; tribalism and, 154
Supreme Islamic Shiʿi Council, 20,
24–25, 108, 122
Sword of Islam, The (Grenada Productions), 33n2

Syria, 7, 23, 43, 45, 81–82, 120, 123;
Amal and, 32, 35; Aoun and, 129;
Baʿth Party and, 15, 19; Gemayel assassination and, 156–57; Gulf War
and, 74–75; Hariri and, 124–28;
Hezbollah and, 34–35; Israeli withdrawal (2000) and, 88–89; League
of Nations mandates and, 11; monitoring groups and, 86; municipal
elections and, 103–5; political ceiling of, 102; postwar conditions and,
152–53; proxy wars and, 72; al-Sadr
and, 19–20; Siniora and, 155; sponsorship of revolutionaries by, 34–35;
Treaty of Brotherhood, Cooperation, and Coordination and, 97–98;
"war of the camps" and, 72–73
Syriac Catholics, 11n1
Syriac Orthodox, 11n1
Syrian Social Nationalist Party
(SSNP), 15, 103, 105

Taʾif accord, 83, 97, 156
taʾifiyya (sectarianism), 121–23, 148
Taklif al-sharʿi (commanded by Allah),
102
al-tashtib (crossing out), 97
tatbir (induced bleeding), 54–55, 61–
63, 118
tawtin (naturalization), 82–83
terrorism, 38, 123, 131; abductions
and, 41–42; car bombs and, 80–81,
127, 131; classification of, 75–77;
embassy attacks and, 71–72, 79; Executive Order 13224 and, 75–76; hi-
jackings and, 42–43; hostages and,
41–44, 73–74, 77, 116, 154; professionalism and, 80; proxy wars and,
83–84; al-Qaeda and, 75–76; Qana
slaughter and, 66, 84–85, 115, 140;
"rules of the game" and, 83–88; September 11 attacks and, 75–76, 132;
suicide bombers and, 6, 71, 80–81,
86; Taʾif accord and, 83; TWA
flight 847 and, 42–43, 77, 79; U.S.

Index

terrorism *(cont.)*
  marine barracks attack and, 6, 71–72, 78
thawrat al-jiyaaᶜ (revolution of the hungry), 105–7, 111
timthiyya (performance), 64–68
tourism, 132, 149, 152
Treaty of Brotherhood, Cooperation, and Coordination, 97–98
tribalism, 154
Tueni, Gibran, 117–18, 131
Tufayli, Subhi, 16, 31, 34, 99–100, 101, 105–6, 111
TWA flight 847, 42–43, 77, 79
Tyre, 3, 80, 105, 109

ʿUbayd, Abdul Karim, 88
ʿulama ("clergy," plural) 40-41; as evil compromisers, 37. See also ʿalim
United Arab Emirates, 137
United Kingdom, 119
United Nations, 38, 42, 122, 134; Annan and, 116; Hariri assassination and, 127, 130–31; hostages and, 73; Interim Force in Lebanon (UNIFIL), 43, 66, 84, 86–88, 141–42, 153–54; Qana slaughter and, 84–85; recent hostilities and, 141–42; sanctions by, 150; Security Council Resolution 1559 and, 132, 139; Security Council Resolution 1701 and, 7–8, 141; Security Council Resolution 1702 and, 142; Security Council Resolution 425 and, 44, 81, 92
United States, 23, 33, 35, 147, 157; Beirut marine barracks attack and, 6, 71–72, 78; blamed by Hezbollah, 37; Central Intelligence Agency (CIA) and, 78; defining terrorism and, 75–77; Department of State, 74, 76; embassy attacks and, 71–72, 78; Executive Order 13224 and, 75–76; Federal Bureau of Investigation (FBI) and, 77; Higgins abduc-

tion and, 43–44; Iran-Contra affair and, 74; Iranian assets and, 41–42; Iraq invasion of, 119; Lebanon-Israel agreement of 1983 and, 41; Litani Operation and, 79–80; monitoring by, 86, 130; Nasrallah sermons and, 67–68; proxy wars and, 72; recent hostilities and, 139, 141; Soviet Union and, 36; Syria and, 35
USA Today, 140

Velayati, Ali-Akbar, 79
violence, 4, 13, 91, 131; abductions and, 41–42; civilian displacement and, 142; Communist assassinations and, 37; disarmament and, 7–8; embassy attacks and, 71–72; fighter wages and, 17–18; Gemayel assassination and, 156–57; guerilla fighters and, 16; Harb al-Tummuz (July war) and, 7; Hariri assassination and, 127–28; Higgins abduction and, 43–44; hostage taking and, 73–74; Hussein (grandson of Muhammad) and, 50–51; Israeli withdrawal (2000) and, 91–93; Litani Operation and, 22–23, 79–80; Operation Grapes of Wrath and, 84; post–civil war period and, 120–23; proxy wars and, 72, 83–84; Qana slaughter and, 66, 84–85, 115, 140; recent hostilities and, 132–43; rituals and, 60–61; "rules of the game" and, 83–88, 134–35; September 11 attacks and, 75–76; Taʾif accord and, 83, 97; terrorism and, 75–79 *(see also* terrorism); TWA flight 847 and, 42–43, 77, 79; U.S. marine barracks attack and, 6, 71–72, 78; "war of the camps" and, 72–73

waʾd al-sadiq (faithful promise), 134–35
waʾd al-dhakar (promise fulfilled), 136

Index

183

Acknowledgments

My first encounter with the Shi'a of Lebanon came in the spring of 1980 in southern Lebanon. I was serving as an unarmed military observer with the United Nations Truce Supervision Organization and heading a small team charged with assisting the United Nations Interim Force in Lebanon (UNIFIL). Early on, Timur Goksel, who was then the Press Information Officer for UNIFIL, and I discussed the renewed activism within the Shi'i community. I also benefited from frequent discussions with the distinguished Chilean diplomat Jaime Holger, who was the political adviser to the commanding general of UNIFIL and who always offered an astute reading of Lebanese politics. It was then the sixth year of the Lebanese civil war—and only two years after Israel's 1978 invasion, the incident which had prompted the Security Council to create UNIFIL. The Palestine Liberation Organization, under Yasser Arafat's leadership, controlled much of Lebanon south of Beirut, but tensions between the PLO and the southern Shi'a were becoming violent, which was a natural concern for UNIFIL. Under UN instructions, I made contact with the local Shi'i leaders, along with two of my very talented colleagues—Desmond Travers of Ireland and Marc Vasco from France—also charter members of our little team. This was two years before Hezbollah would emerge in Lebanon, so I met frequently with members of the inchoate Amal movement, led nationally by Nabih Berri, and by the late Daoud Suleiman Daoud in the South. For more than a year I enjoyed an unusually privileged, if fortuitous, entree to local Shi'i politics. This was a protean moment in local Shi'i politics. Within a couple of years, growing suspicion toward the United States and the radicalization of Shi'i politics, would make access much more difficult, and even for a period foolhardly. Over the course of the past quarter century, however, I have been able to return Lebanon frequently, sometimes even to continue conversations with the children of the men and women with whom the conversations first began.

From the start, I was more interested in understanding political trends and perspectives than in gathering names, and I usually promised my interlocutors that I would not publish their names unless they agreed to speak on the public record. If I had not respected this ground rule in those early days, and ever since, my access to Shi'i politics would have been much more limited. I would like to thank two old friends who were extremely generous teachers. One, a Christian of gentle spirit but firm integrity, comes from a Lebanese village on the Israeli border; he taught me a tremendous amount about the complex culture of the region. He is now one of the most respected generals in Lebanon. Another officer, I shall call him Abu Hamudi, became an especially dear friend. I could always trust him to give me straight answers, and during dangerous times he demonstrated his willingness to risk his life to protect mine. Abu Hamudi died far too young—from a relentless disease—in 2004. He was a man of moderate views who, while very proud of being Lebanese, was also openly frustrated by Lebanon's sometimes stultifying, and too often corrupt, political system. I don't expect that Abu Hamudi would have agreed with every word in this little book, but I would like to think that he would find this an honest account of the leading Shi'i political party in Lebanon—Hezbollah.

Acknowledgments

Over the course of many visits to Lebanon, I have benefited from hundreds of conversations with other Lebanese colleagues, friends, intellectuals, journalists, and business people. Here I wish simply to acknowledge a general debt, and to promise that I will find more private occasions to extent my gratitude.

I would like to note that substantial parts of chapter 3 were first published as "Ritual, Blood, and Shiite Identity," *Drama Review* 49, no. 4 (Winter 2005), and are used here with permission. Also, some parts of chapters 1 and 2 have appeared, in rather different form, in *Hizballah of Lebanon: From Radical Idealism to Mundane Politics* (New York: Council on Foreign Relations, 1999), and in "Hizballah: From Radicalism to Pragmatism," *Middle East Policy* 5, no. 4 (January 1998); material from both sources are used here with permission. The Hezbollah "Open Letter," discussed in chapter 2, was first published in English in my own *Amal and the Shiʿa: Struggle for the Soul of Lebanon* (Austin: University of Texas Press, 1987).

I would like to thank Rita Bernhard for being a wonderful copy-editor. Rita often amazed me not only with her competence, but also by her ability to turn copy around so quickly that I sometimes wished she would slow down. Tobiah Waldron prepared a comprehensive, even perceptive index, which I am confident readers will find unusually useful. The extraordinary efforts of the Princeton University Press team may not pass unheralded. Finally, I must thank DLN and ATN for making my *dunya* complete.